Thomas K. Johnson

The Protester, the Dissident, and the Christian

World of Theology Series

Published by the Theological Commission of the World Evangelical Alliance

Volume 19

Thomas K. Johnson

The Protester, the Dissident, and the Christian

Essays on Human Rights and Religion

Foreword by C. Holland Taylor

Appendix by Pavel Hošek

WIPF & STOCK · Eugene, Oregon

Wipf and Stock Publishers
199 W 8th Ave, Suite 3
Eugene, OR 97401

The Protester, the Dissident, and the Christian
Essays on Human Rights and Religion
By Johnson, Thomas K. and Taylor, C. Holland
Copyright © 2021 Verlag für Kultur und Wissenschaft Culture and Science Publ. All rights reserved
Softcover ISBN-13: 978-1-6667-0441-9
Hardcover ISBN-13: 978-1-6667-0442-6
Publication date 3/4/2021
Previously published by Verlag für Kultur und Wissenschaft Culture and Science Publ., 2021

Contents

Preface

As Thomas Schirrmacher has abundantly documented in *Human Rights: Promise and Reality,* the great 1948 Universal Declaration of Human Rights (UDHR) hovers over humanity as an unfulfilled promise.[1] Terrible abuses of ordinary people, even whole groups of ordinary people, continue without end. After the Holocaust millions cried "Never again!" leading most of the world to affirm the UDHR. But today much of that same world ignores their cry. Genocide, crimes against humanity, persecution, and widespread discrimination are as common as the rising of the sun. Some protest vigorously, but millions face such horrible oppression they cannot raise their voices.

This book arises from my attempts over the last 25 years to raise the profile of this tragedy while also promoting clear thinking about human rights. Bad theology, bad philosophy, and bad political theory have led to terrible real-world results for ordinary people; I can only hope that better ideas might lead to better results. If you disagree with the ideas in this book, please respond by writing something far better in defense of the rights of our neighbors. Many of these essays were initially speeches that allowed responses from the audience.

It is the assumption of this book that human rights are real, arising from the reality of human dignity, a primordial reality known with certainty to all, prior to religious or theoretical explanation, though denied by sociopaths and ideologues. Because of this ontological reality, morally sane people immediately sense the ring of truth when Jesus taught us to love our neighbors as ourselves and to do unto others as we would have them do onto us. This naturally known universal ethical rule (described by many religious and philosophical teachers) provides the background and backbone for real human rights; it also provides the basis to question ideologies and pseudo-human rights claims.

This universal standard also provides the background for Jesus' specific test for the authenticity of religion. He said, "By this everyone will know that you are my disciples, if you love one another" (John 13:35). The ancient universal standard has become, by this declaration, the specific standard for recognizing true religion, "discipleship" in the language of

---

[1]   Thomas Schirrmacher, *Human Rights: Promise and Reality,* vol. 15, World Evangelical Alliance Global Issues Series (Bonn: VKW, 2014); https://iirf.eu/journal-books/global-issues-series/human-rights-18/.

Christian theology. This is the link between human rights and authentic faith. There is properly an organic connection between the duty of all humanity to protect the rights of their neighbors and the duty of a religious community to love their fellow believers. We should think in terms of concentric circles: In the inner circle we must demonstrate the authenticity of our religion by love for the members of our religious community; in the outer circle we demonstrate our humanity when we protect the rights of others.

It is a mistake to confuse the two circles. The expectation that a state should act like a church or that a church should act like a state has contributed to great tragedies. Protecting rights is a proper ethical language for states, including state education and state health care. Self-sacrificial love is the right moral language for the close bonds formed by shared prayer and worship. Nevertheless, recognizing the humanity of the other is the connection between protecting human rights in the outer circle of public institutions and practicing true spirituality in the inner circle of our religious communities.

Regardless of your religion or political orientation, please join me in thinking deeply about protecting the most vulnerable of our neighbors.

To encourage further study, we have included many links in the footnotes. If you are reading this book in an electronic format, the links should be active, allowing you to reach the texts cited by clicking. We have printed the links for the benefit of readers using printed versions of this book, allowing you to type the info into a browser to find the sources.

Foreword

In his book *The Protester, the Dissident and the Christian*, Thomas K. Johnson examines an issue of paramount importance — human rights — through the complex and intersecting lenses of Protestant and medieval Thomistic theology, ethical and political philosophy, and geopolitics, augmented by a healthy dose of common sense.

A respected Evangelical scholar, Dr. Johnson makes a strong case not only for the continued relevance of Christian theology to the global human rights endeavor, but indeed, for the necessity to ground this endeavor in what C.S. Lewis, in *The Abolition of Man*, described as "the absolute values of the *Tao*."

In recent decades, liberal democracies in North America and Europe — once home to a majority of the world's Christian population — have grown increasingly secular, giving rise to immense cultural and political rifts. On one side stand proponents of a secular ideology whose cultural, economic and political power verges upon hegemony in much of the West. On the other side of this gulf stand those who embrace more traditional values, including many Christians, Orthodox Jews and Muslims.

This situation is exacerbated by recent developments in human rights advocacy and Western political discourse. The concept of human rights has acquired such enormous cultural and moral authority in the West that novel rights claims have proliferated dramatically in recent decades.

The post-9/11 re-emergence of "identity politics" in the West reflects and accelerates this phenomenon by fostering a dynamic in which a kaleidoscopic array of "intersectional groups" insist that their grievances be acknowledged, and their demands met, by governments and society at large.

Post-war Western societies were uniquely successful in providing an even-handed and effective framework within which diverse identity groups and worldviews could contend for influence and peacefully co-exist. However, the rapidly accelerating polarization of Europe and the United States suggests that a militant, post-modern "hypertrophied" secularism — hostile to the values traditionally associated with Western humanism and Christian democracy, including the enlightenment's veneration of reason and science — can no longer play this role either in the West or upon the world stage.

Given these circumstances, how can we effectively address the polarization that threatens to undo the unique achievements of Western civilization, which helped give birth to a rules-based international order founded upon respect for the equal rights and dignity of every human being?

Leaders of the global Humanitarian Islam movement believe that the answer lies in a search for shared civilizational values that may serve as the basis of peaceful coexistence, by fostering solidarity and respect among the diverse people, cultures and nations of the world. As one of the largest faith communities on earth, Evangelical Christians have a vital role to play in this endeavor.

Just as Evangelicals once led successful "revolutionary movements" to abolish slavery in the 19th century and to establish freedom of conscience, so Evangelical Christians today — in the West *and* the Global South — may draw upon their rich heritage to help strengthen and preserve a rules-based international order founded upon universal ethics and humanitarian values.

This book is a valuable contribution to that effort.

C. Holland Taylor
Gerakan Pemuda Ansor Emissary to the United Nations, Americas and Europe
Co-chair, Humanitarian Islam/World Evangelical Alliance Joint Working Group

The Protester, the Dissident, and the Christian[2]

The protests and riots that have exploded in the United States and even globally since the death of George Floyd on May 25, 2020, have taken my mind back to 2011, a year in which *Time* magazine declared "The Protester" to be its person of the year.[3] Few years in recorded history before 2011 were so strongly characterized by a sense that something is terribly wrong with the whole world. On the streets of Tunis, Cairo, Tripoli, Athens, Damascus, New York, Beijing, and London, the participants in the Arab Spring and Occupy Wall Street uprisings publicly encouraged each other across the globe. Around the world, people were angry over the perception that their friends, neighbors, and fellow citizens were being treated unjustly. The events sparking the protests were so diverse as to resist a unified description. It is hard to say whether any good results came from some of the efforts; revolutions often end poorly.

The editors of *Time* magazine could not know that their announcement would be upstaged four days later. One of the most admired revolutionaries of recent history died on December 18, 2011: Vaclav Havel, the prominent author and dissident who contributed significantly to the fall of communism in 1989 and subsequently became the first democratic president of the Czech Republic. Havel's Velvet Revolution ended well, leading to decades of freedom and economic growth.[4]

---

2   This essay originated as a sermon at the International Church of Prague on January 1, 2012. It was then published in 2012 as a booklet by Martin Bucer Seminary as MBS Text 168 (2012), https://www.bucer.de/fileadmin/_migrated/tx_org/mbstexte168_b.pdf. Revised versions were published by the World Reformed Fellowship in September, 2020, https://wrf.global/blog/blog-2/christian-life/the-protester-the-dissident-and-the-christian, and by the *Evangelical Review of Theology* in November, 2020, https://theology.worldea.org/wp-content/uploads/2020/10/ERT-44-4.pdf.

3   *Time* magazine named "The Protester" as its 2011 Person of the Year on 14 December 2011. See Rick Stengel, "Person of the Year Introduction," http://content.time.com/time/specials/packages/article/0,28804,2101745_2102139,00.html.

4   Havel's state funeral was held on December 23, 2011, at Saint Vitus Cathedral in Prague, Czech Republic, after three days of official public mourning. The end of communism in which he played a leading role was called the "Velvet Revolution" because it was non-violent. Critics of this term argue that a change of government without violence is not a true revolution.

I have used two distinct though overlapping terms here: *protester* and *dissident*. A dissident is a long-term opponent of an established religious or political institution. Dissidents may be either open or very reserved about expressing their opposition to the establishment. Protesters take part in a public demonstration in response to a particular event or policy. Many protesters seek only a specific policy change, not a fundamental change in a government or religion, so they are not dissidents. On the other hand, dissidents who express their desires in an underground manner are not generally considered protesters, since protests are public events.

I have long pondered, as far back as the race riots of 1968, how Jesus would relate to protests and revolutionary rhetoric. Wasn't Jesus himself a dissident who engaged in years of conflict with the authorities of his time? Isn't Palm Sunday a global celebration of the most famous protest ever, Jesus' ride into Jerusalem on a donkey to cleanse a corrupt temple? Was not Jesus' unjust death the greatest unveiling of the depth of dishonesty and corruption to which religious and political authorities can fall?

Now that George Floyd's death and the deaths of others have provoked millions to engage in a new round of protests against racism and discrimination, I am again asking, "What would Jesus do?" However, we will not find a tweet-sized answer to this question.

The biblical message pushes us to be radicals, deeply dissatisfied with our societies as they currently exist. The biblical message is much more than a message of protest against the deep-seated evils of our world, but it should not be less. Similarly, although it should also be many more things, the Christian community should not be less than a community of dissidents, talking about what is wrong with our world and offering solutions. And we should especially be offering a message of reconciliation with God and with our neighbors to our fellow dissidents who do not yet believe in Christ.

In that spirit, I will propose some suggestions, first to protesters and dissidents and then to church members.

The Hidden Godward Assumptions of Dissidents and Protesters

Protests and dissident movements start with several convictions that might remain hidden, though a few may articulate them openly. I call these assumptions "Godward," because, I contend, these convictions are God-given even among people who are atheists or uncertain about what they believe about God.

1. Though we are sometimes mistaken in our views, we know that there exists a standard of right and wrong that is above our feelings; on this basis we see that certain things are wrong.

When people argue, whether in private or on the streets, there is inevitably an appeal, perhaps implicit, to an ethical standard by which our actions may be judged. When people are of the same religion, they may refer to a religious text and say, "the Bible says . . ." or "the Koran says . . ." When people do not share a religion, the norm referenced may be less explicit; nevertheless, it is crucial. Normal people do not say, "There are no standards, so do what you want." When we engage in debate, we are implicitly claiming, "According to the standards which we all know, I am right and you are wrong;" we never say, "Let's fight like animals."[5] This unwritten standard has traditionally been called the natural moral law, sometimes more simply just natural law. Protest movements are screams for people to pay attention to this universal standard.

Within Christianity, the natural moral law is seen as a dimension of creation, part of how our minds have been fashioned in the image of the divine Mind, such that we can hardly avoid distinguishing between right and wrong. Globally, people make similar assumptions about general standards of right and wrong, even across diverse cultures.[6] Christian theology claims that this natural moral law is a prominent theme in God's ongoing general revelation, God's speech which comes to humanity in multiple ways throughout his creation. The result is that most people know basic principles about right and wrong even if they cannot explain this knowledge. Protesters and dissidents depend on this knowledge.

---

5   This analysis of moral discourse is heavily dependent on C. S. Lewis, especially *Mere Christianity* (London and Glasgow: Collins, 1952), 15–26. For an assessment of Lewis on this topic, see Thomas K. Johnson, *Natural Law Ethics: An Evangelical Proposal* (Bonn: VKW, 2005), 85–105, available at https://www.academia.edu/ 36884239/Natural_Law_Ethics_An_Evangelical_Proposal.

6   For a mid-twentieth-century study of this topic, see C. S. Lewis, *The Abolition of Man* (Oxford: Oxford University Press, 1943), appendix: "Illustrations of the Tao." For a late-twentieth-century effort, see the *Declaration Toward a Global Ethic* (Chicago: Parliament of the World's Religions, 1993); https://www.global-ethic.org/ declaration-toward-a-global-ethic/. For a more recent, official Roman Catholic discussion of this theme, see *In Search of a Global Ethic: A New Look at the Natural Law* (International Theological Commission of the Congregation for the Doctrine of the Faith, 2009 in French and Italian, 2013 in English); http://www.vatican.va/ roman_curia/congregations/cfaith/cti_documents/rc_con_cfaith_doc_20090520 _legge-naturale_en.html.

2. There is something special about human beings; people have dignity that is worthy of respect, justice, and care.

Within Christian and Jewish teaching, this is called the image of God in humans. The term recalls the Genesis creation account: "God created mankind in his own image, in the image of God he created them; male and female he created them" (Genesis 1:27). We might call it the reflection of divine dignity in the other. Whether or not they are familiar with this religious teaching, morally healthy people recognize something about people that is different from other things. I often put my feet on my desk when I am writing (an old leg injury makes this more comfortable); it would be terribly wrong for me to put my feet on another human being, regardless of that person's race, politics, or religion.

Human uniqueness is assumed by protesters, and this assumption merits frequent mention. This fact speaks to the dignity of the people whose fundamental rights have been robbed, but it also speaks to the dignity of the protester, as well as the dignity of the people addressed by a protest: public authorities and voters. The complex human communications in protests, then, take place among people with God-given dignity and a God-given sense of right and wrong.

3. There are many things in every society that are terribly wrong; these wrongs need to be criticized and changed. But we must be careful, because misguided efforts to achieve change can easily make things even more wrong.

Morally sensitive people come to the conclusion that things around them are horribly wrong because of the Godward assumptions discussed above. The universal moral standard and our awareness of God-given dignity provide the conditions that make morally serious protesting possible. However, not every attempt to criticize or change society leads to good results. Terrible mistakes with devasting results are easy to commit.

Before moving to the former Soviet Union in 1994, I read several books by Karl Marx. I saw the differences between Marx's own teaching and the actual practice of communism. This allowed me a window into the disillusionment and despair that many people felt after communism failed.

Marx thought most people were miserable because of their alienation from themselves, their work, and their neighbors. In the broadest terms, he promised that a revolutionary change of economic relations and the end of economic classes would bring an end to alienation. Though revolutionaries claiming to follow Marx came into power in 1917 (in Russia) and again after World War II in 1945 to 1948 (across much of Eastern Europe), their revolutions did not fulfil that promise. Though some poverty was reduced and some people attained a low degree of economic security, these gains came at the cost of despotic control by paranoid secret police and the loss of the freedoms of speech and religion, with millions severely persecuted or killed. Everyone was afraid their friend or relative would report them to the police for something they said in private.

Not only did the treatment (communism) not fit the diagnosis (Marxist thought), the diagnosis included fatal mistakes. Long before the end of European communism in 1989, most people on both sides of the Iron Curtain knew that communism dramatically increased human alienation and suffering. Marx and the communists ignored what St. Augustine described as the "lust for domination" (*libido dominandi*)[7] or what Friedrich Nietzsche described as the "will to power" (*der Wille zur Macht*).[8]

Such philosophical mistakes inherent in Marxism and communism turned hope for a better future into suffering and despair, but the religious mistake was even more distorted. The proletariat, the working class, was described as something like a godlike savior that would deliver society from the evils of the upper class or bourgeoisie, whereas belief in God was an opiate that prevented the proletariat from seizing control to create a new society. I come from a working-class family and know many wonderful people, but they do not have the godlike ability to create a fundamentally new society. This profound theological error led to catastrophe in the many countries that were controlled by communism. Theology matters.

Protesters, dissidents, and revolutionaries build on convictions which I have described as Godward: convictions about a standard of right and wrong, about human dignity, and about the religious desire to help people who are suffering indignity and injustice. So did Marx and the early communists! But massive mistakes about religion and philosophy led to human disaster. Unfortunately, it has been my experience that protesters and dissidents sometimes resist discussing these matters, perhaps because their anger at injustice is so hot.

In 2011, I gave a lecture about human rights for a group of Belarusian pro-democracy dissidents who were in exile from their homeland, out of reach from the authoritarian dictator Aleksandr Lukashenko (another target of the 2020 round of protests). My understanding of human rights is organically tied to normal Christian beliefs about creation, the fall, and even the Incarnation, so I did not avoid those topics. I knew that some of the dissidents were Christians. But I felt tension in the room, even

---

[7]   Augustine's phrase appears in the preface to book 1 of *The City of God*.
[8]   Nietzsche used this phrase in various essays. For example, in *Beyond Good and Evil*, paragraph 13, he wrote, "Life itself is will to power."

resistance, when I moved from the political level of hating totalitarianism to the level of discussing a universal moral law and the ultimate source of human dignity — God. People are sometimes frightened to connect political convictions with convictions about human nature and the nature of the universe, as I have just done. I soon perceived that for these dissidents, organized religion was linked with an oppressive government. That is a serious problem which merits our attention. Inauthentic religion easily gets everything wrong in relation to the state, as Jesus experienced at the end of his earthly life.

The Christian Dissident's Mind

What I have said thus far was intended for protesters and dissidents who have not yet clarified their relationship with the Christian message. Now I will address people who understand themselves as Christians with four themes that should prepare us to become more effective Christian dissidents and to engage in thoughtful Christian proclamation in the midst of our quests for justice.

1. The Christian can take the social criticism of the protester and go deeper, to articulate God's criticism of sinful humanity. Injustices in society are the result of sin, including not recognizing God.
     The protester and the dissident start with the conviction that something in society is profoundly wrong. Those who read the Bible should notice the similarity to the Old Testament prophets, many of whom had highly conflicted relationships with society. Some 2,700 years ago, Amos proclaimed, "This is what the Lord says: 'For three sins of Gaza, even for four, I will not turn back my wrath. Because she took captive whole communities and sold them to Edom'" (Amos 1:6). Amos assumed that all normal people know that kidnapping and slave trading are atrocities, because people have a conscience informed by the universal moral law. What Amos pointedly added to his description, beyond what most protesters talk about, is the wrath of God. God is angry when people are mistreated.
     On some occasions, the prophets criticized Israel and Judah based on the law of Moses. But on other occasions, such as in Amos 1, they spoke to the surrounding nations based on moral standards known to everyone, regardless of the religions the peoples followed. What I said above about an unwritten standard can be derived from Amos. This is where the proclamations of protesters and dissidents are frequently deficient; in spite of great moral courage, some lack the spiritual courage to recognize we are

sinners before God. We all easily ignore the greatest injustice against Persons in the universe, that people ignore the dignity of God.

We Christians should borrow a page from other protesters and dissidents to become much more courageous about confronting injustices in our world. However, if we accept Amos as a role model, we need to add a much deeper level to our social criticism. Christian dissidents and protesters need to address the deepest level of the problem: sin, alienation from God, and even the wrath of God. If we do this, there will be no separation of our Christian proclamation from our concerns as social dissidents.

2. The Christian can take the hope proclaimed by the protester and dissident and go deeper to proclaim our ultimate political hope, a new heaven and a new earth.

People always look for a source of hope and courage that is based on a promise. Even when despair and disillusionment threaten, people can find hope for a better future so long as they have at least a flimsy promise. The human heart can hardly resist trusting in promises. At the core of every protest and dissident movement is a promise of a better future, whether for us or for our children.

Social and political hope is both precious and fragile. Hope empowers people to work toward a better future, even if it will cost blood, sweat, and tears. Though I am deeply concerned about deceptive hope, I think hope can be a tool of God's common grace to bring about a more prosperous, free, and just future. When some of my ancestors lived under conditions of terrible poverty, hope gave them the courage to bring about a better future.

Recognizing the depth of sin and foolishness should not destroy political hope. The real threat to hope comes from confusing secondary hope with ultimate hope. As Christians we should trust in God's promise that he will give us a new heaven and a new earth (Revelation 21:1). At that time, "He will wipe every tear from their eyes. There will be no more death or mourning or crying or pain, for the old order of things has passed away" (21:4). This is our ultimate hope in Christ. We believe it will come after the end of history, when, as we say in the Apostles' Creed, Jesus will come as the Judge of the living and the dead.

If people do not place their hope in God, they continually place their ultimate hope in the promises of a human savior. Already in the time of Jesus, some of the Jews put too much hope in a political savior who would free them from the hated Roman Empire. Some of the worst events in the twentieth century were caused by people putting ultimate hope in a secular savior. Hitler, Stalin, and Mao are prime examples.

Death and destruction follow when people trust the promises of a mere human as if he were a divine Messiah.

We Christians should boldly say that no leader or ideology can bring heaven to earth, but that does not mean we simply accept the world as it is. Our ultimate hope, based in God's promise of a new heaven and a new earth, should give us hope for improvements in this age.

Only Jesus will wipe away every tear, but we can wipe away some tears. Only Jesus will bring the end of mourning and pain, but we can reduce mourning and pain. Jesus is the only ultimate Victor over injustice, but perhaps we can reduce human trafficking, racial discrimination, and religious persecution. And all our efforts to change things in this world should stand as a sign and symbol that Jesus will ultimately wipe away every tear and punish every injustice. We must protest injustice as a sign that Jesus will ultimately end all injustice. And while we protest and work for change, we must always say clearly that our limited efforts point to the real and eternal hope, that Jesus is the ultimate Savior.

3. The Christian can describe the body of Christ as an alternate, dissident community that points to our eternal hope.

It is characteristic of dissident movements to form alternative communities with their own internal cultures. For example, the dissidents in communist Czechoslovakia had their own foundational document (Charter 77), their own small group meetings, their own underground literature, and even their own conflicts and differences of opinion. Consider the people who gathered in Hahrir Square in Cairo during the 2011 protests against Egyptian President Hosni Mubarak: the estimated 50,000 people quickly developed their own internal culture, with norms, customs, and organization. Once people perceive their society to be fundamentally flawed, they very naturally form an alternate society, a counterculture.

Already in the first century, the basic Christian confession referenced Christians' relation to their society. Roman society said, "Caesar is Lord;" the Christians said, "Jesus is Lord." With these words they not only described their trust in Jesus; they also said they did not trust in the religious promise at the core of the Roman Empire, the religious ideology that shaped the society. The New Testament church became a counterculture.

The counterculture they formed, however, was not disconnected from their world; rather, a central task of the church is always to carry the word of God's judgment and of God's grace into society. Such a thoughtful interaction with one's surrounding society includes recognizing what is good in a society. The early Christians recognized the goods brought by the Roman Empire, such as roads, law enforcement, and a common language, that helped people and families to flourish. They also saw these benefits of the Roman Empire as part of the God-given *kairos*, the appointed time for taking the gospel to the nations. Then and now, believing in Jesus makes us an alternative community with a mission.

In the Western world, we have a history of mistakes in this matter. I grew up in a Dutch community in the U.S. state of Michigan, where the church was frequently seen as providing the moral coherence for society. As a result, we sometimes lacked a clear sense of where we needed to be dissidents in relation to our society. This was part of the lingering heritage of Christendom, dating back to the time of Constantine. There were problems with this model of faith and society: confessing faith in Jesus was too much like promising to be a good citizen. The element of rejecting the false standards and false messiahs of the world was sometimes weak, though a strong sense that the world needed Jesus provided a corrective.

As soon as we describe the church as a dissident community, with its own standards and way of life, we encounter a recurring problem. Consider the words of Nietzsche, one of my favorite atheists: "If they want me to believe in their redeemer, they should look like redeemed people." For a long time, I thought Nietzsche was right. But we have this problem: as Christians, we want to look like something we are not. We want to pretend to already be fully redeemed when in fact we are still in process. To be honest, we still find incidents of injustice, abuse, and betrayal occurring among us. We are in the process of being redeemed, but that process will not be complete until Jesus returns.

What makes us Christians a dissident people is our belief that Jesus is Lord, which means there is no other lord, savior, or messiah. And we accept the message that Jesus is Lord with universal intent, meaning that Jesus is the Messiah whom everyone needs. We are carriers of this message of hope for all the world.

4. Like every dissident community, we want to make massive changes in our entire society; we also want to preach the gospel to all.

If the dissident starts with the conviction that something is fundamentally wrong in society, then the dissident community wants to bring about real changes. This is true of almost every dissident movement around the world. It is their defining quality. They desire to contribute to a better future.

This is also true for us as a Christian community. Our dissident agenda should be on two levels, a moral level and a spiritual level. For example, we long to dramatically reduce human trafficking, divorce, abortion, religious persecution, and racism; we also want people to know God through faith in Jesus. Throughout Christian history, Christians have often recognized this two-sided calling: to declare peace with God while also making significant contributions to society.

Whether our social contribution is to write treatises on the concept of human dignity, to adopt a child, or to start a local business, our two-sided agenda flows from the two-part revelation of God: his general revelation of a universal standard and of human dignity makes humane communities possible in this world, while his special revelation in the Bible proclaims redemption in Christ. As Christians, we want to make it possible for people to come to real faith in Jesus; as a dissident Christian community, we seek to produce positive changes in our societies. Our world needs a new generation who are both preachers and dissidents.

Our Assignment

In conclusion, I propose this "to do" list for Christians and other dissidents:

1. Recognize that our world is deeply flawed. This is the starting point for any dissident or protester.
2. Accept your role as a dissident in relation to society.
3. Consider that honest protests are only possible on the basis of what God is already doing, namely, giving us the universal moral law and human dignity.
4. Develop courage to talk comfortably about our central Christian convictions as the foundation for being truly serious dissidents.
5. Identify ways in which you can both protest against and contribute to your society.
6. Confess that our churches have made serious mistakes about how to address the injustices of our world, compelling us to pursue improvements.

May we have the courage to function as serious Christian protesters and dissidents, so that our lives may point back to the human dignity given in creation and point forward toward the final end of alienation and injustice, our ultimate hope.

Why Study Martin Luther King?

The "Letter from a Birmingham Jail" and Christian Human Rights Principles[9]

On Martin Luther King Day 2019 (an official U.S. holiday), I listened to an inspiring podcast. It was very informative, with generous quotations from Dr. King. The hearts of the people who organized the podcast were clearly moved by King's speeches, such as "I Have a Dream," and now they were digging deeply into King's moral philosophy.[10] As I listened, one peculiarity caught my ear: the commentator, who spoke fluid, sophisticated English, struggled to pronounce certain old names that appear in King's famous 1963 "Letter from a Birmingham Jail." The commentator seemed not to recognize biblical names such as Shadrach, Meshach, and Abednego. Similarly, the name of Thomas Aquinas got stuck on his tongue. Yet the commentator was clearly searching; he was searching, I believe, not only for how to pronounce ancient names. Beyond that he was searching for intellectual resources that might provide new courage and direction for human rights efforts, perhaps sensing the weaknesses of today's human rights discourse.

---

[9] This essay is a revised version of a speech entitled "Martin Luther King and Those Wonderful Old Names!

The 'Letter from a Birmingham Jail' and Christian Human Rights Resources," given at the first annual International Human Rights Conference in Prague, Czech Republic, on March 7, 2019, hosted by Anglo-American University, Norwich University, and Post Bellum. Websites:

– Anglo-American University, https://www.aauni.edu/.

– Norwich University, http://www.norwich.edu/.

– Post Bellum, https://www.postbellum.cz/english/.

Previous versions of this essay were published as "Martin Luther King and those Wonderful Old Names," by Martin Bucer Seminary, MBS Text 192 (2019), https://www.bucer.org/en/resources/resources/details/mbs-texte-192-2019-mar tin-luther-king-and-those-wonderful-old-names.html, and as WEA Bulletin 5, October 2019, https://worldea.org/wp-content/uploads/2020/06/WEA-DTC-Bulle-tin-engl_small_5a_Oct-2019.pdf.

[10] Martin Luther King's most famous speech, "I Have a Dream," was given during a March on Washington (DC) on August 28, 1963. The text of his speech can be found here: https://www.americanrhetoric.com/speeches/mlkihaveadream.htm. A video of the event, with subtitles, is available here: https://www.youtube.com/watch?v=vP4iY1TtS3s.

This commentator's lack of familiarity with these old names seems to represent many a person's unfamiliarity with how the Judeo-Christian tradition has been fueling, really propelling, human rights thought and action for centuries. In contrast with some in our time, when Dr. King wrote his "Letter from a Birmingham Jail," the intellectual manifesto of the American civil rights movement, he demonstrated a deep and wide-ranging familiarity with the primary texts of Judeo-Christian ethics. This is worthy of our attention. The way in which King appropriated these old resources provided history-changing courage and direction to the civil rights movement. It is well worth our time to explore Dr. King's resources to see if we too can find courage and direction.[11]

King's letter addresses both the political and religious spheres, never separating faith and public philosophy. It is one of the most important American political texts of the twentieth century, but it is also a deeply spiritual text, written by a Christian minister and addressed to American religious communities. It is a call for the legal and political protection of human rights, as well as a plea for spiritual renewal in the churches and synagogues. The organic relatedness of the religious and political spheres is found in the sources Dr. King used, which is one of the reasons why these sources merit our attention.

1. The Prophets

King's first mention of old religious sources in this letter is to the eighth-century prophets who "left their little villages and carried their 'thus saith the Lord' far beyond the boundaries of their hometowns." Later he quoted the prophet Amos, "Let justice roll down like waters and righteousness like a mighty stream," after asking if Amos was an extremist (as some were calling Dr. King) because of his appeal for justice.

The prophets King had in mind, from about 800 BC to about 700 BC, spoke to Israel, Judah, and the surrounding nations. Sometimes they

---

[11]   The letter was dated April 16, 1963. A good text is found here: https://www.af rica.upenn.edu/Articles_Gen/Letter_Birmingham.html. Though I am recommending the study of King's famous letter and the sources King used, this is not a complete endorsement of King as a role model. There are serious allegations that he was sexually unfaithful to his wife and that he plagiarized as a student. He did not always affirm some standard Christian beliefs, and his proposals regarding the Vietnam War may have been influenced by members of the Communist Party, USA. See Joe Carter, "9 Things You Should Know About Martin Luther King, Jr.," The Gospel Coalition, January 19, 2014. https://www.thegospelcoalition.org/ar ticle/9-things-you-should-know-about-martin-luther-king-jr-2.

promised God's future redemption, but King was especially thinking about how writers such as Amos, Hosea, Isaiah, and Micah exposed the evils of their time, what we today call human rights abuses. Amos was typical in this regard and perhaps a favorite of Dr. King. Foreshadowing journalists of a later era, Amos described atrocities and pronounced doom on the perpetrators.

For example, Amos claims:

> "This is what the Lord says:
> 'For three sins of Gaza, even for four, I will not relent.
> Because she took captive whole communities and sold them to Edom,
> I will send fire on the walls of Gaza that will consume her fortresses.'"[12]

At that time, Edom was the home of slave traders. The people of Gaza were capturing "whole communities" to sell them as slaves. In the name of God, Amos predicted justice.

Amos also wrote:

> "This is what the Lord says:
> 'For three sins of Ammon, even for four, I will not relent.
> Because he ripped open the pregnant women of Gilead to extend his borders.'"[13]

In a war of expansion, the people of Ammon committed unspeakable crimes. Words fail us in light of what they did. In the name of God, Amos again predicted justice.

In several such brief reports, Amos exposed the atrocities of the nations surrounding Israel and Judah. The texts make us expect the citizens of Israel and Judah to applaud such condemnations, since the people of Israel and Judah are portrayed as proud of their moral and religious superiority to the less enlightened nations. Doubtless to the horror of his audience, Amos then addressed the sins of Israel in terms that were equally as colorful and confrontational:

> "This is what the Lord says:
> 'For three sins of Israel, even for four, I will not relent.
> They sell the innocent for silver, and the needy for a pair of sandals.
> They trample on the heads of the poor as on the dust of the ground and deny justice to the oppressed.'"[14]

---

[12]   Amos 1:6 - 7 NIV.
[13]   Amos 1:13 NIV.
[14]   Amos 2:6 - 7 NIV.

The details are not clear, but obviously the powerful were oppressing and perhaps selling the poor. Since sandals were sometimes used symbolically to confirm property transactions, the abuse may have included stealing farmland from the poor, forcing the poor into greater poverty or even starvation. The valuable religious and moral identity of Israel did not restrain them from crimes against humanity.

The ancient prophets did not speak the language of political science. They did not use the terms "civil rights" or "human rights abuses" or precisely delimit state actors from non-state actors. They did not articulate a theory of democracy. They talked about people abusing people. When Dr. King exposed the sins of racial discrimination in his day, he was standing on the shoulders of the prophets, little-known people from antiquity who addressed the evils of kings, empires, and religious people in the name of God. Those prophets number among our deepest sources for developing a truly serious way of talking about human rights abuses.

There is an important but sometimes implicit ethical theme found in King and in the prophets that merits explicit mention in our era of heightened awareness of the cultural relativity of moral rules. The central moral problem addressed by Dr. King was that members of his black community, many of whom were descendants of slaves, were not treated fairly by the majority (and wealthier) white community. His people faced frequent discrimination or exclusion regarding schools, businesses, jobs, buses, restaurants, and many other social situations. Another way of describing this problem was that the white community had a clear set of moral standards for how they treated each other, but this set of moral standards was culturally limited to their own community and did not apply to other people groups, especially not to those whom they called "negroes." Race-based discrimination was an organic part of a type of cultural moral relativism, the idea that moral rules are not binding on all human interactions, only on interactions with people within one's own culture.[15] A crucial

---

[15]   We normally contrast moral relativism with moral absolutism (or moral universalism). Moral absolutism says there are moral rules that apply to all people universally, regardless of race, culture, or nationality. Moral relativism claims there are no absolute moral rules, only relative moral rules. There are two main types of moral relativism, cultural relativism and individual relativism. Cultural relativism claims that right and wrong are dependent on the culture within which an action occurs, such that one culture might properly affirm racism while another culture properly rejects racism as morally wrong. Individual relativism claims that right and wrong are dependent on the individual acting, so that each person must decide for himself/herself what is right and what is wrong; if individual relativism is true, each person may properly decide if racism is good or if racism is evil.

assumption of the civil rights movement is that there is one set of moral rules that applies to all human interactions, regardless of the situation, race, color, or culture of the people interacting. The very existence of the civil rights movement in which Dr. King was a leader was an appeal to a universal moral law, which King thought everyone should be able to recognize.

This appeal to a universal moral law was especially evident in the quotations from the prophet Amos. Amos transparently identified himself as rooted in Jewish religion and culture, but he spoke to people from multiple other religions and cultures (such as Ammon and Gaza) about how they treated people from still other cultures and religions. He appealed to a universal moral law that should apply to all human interactions and which all should be able to recognize regardless of their culture and beliefs. The appeal to a universal moral law which King appropriated was part of the Judeo-Christian moral tradition, but it was far more than an appropriation of one particular religious tradition. It was a claim that regardless of religion, culture, or tradition, all people know much about right and wrong, including knowing that racism and segregation are morally wrong.

There are some themes in the ancient prophets which I find profoundly disturbing. First, the prophets wrote as if the people committing the atrocities knew that their actions were horribly wrong. A lack of moral information was not the problem! According to Amos, the people in power knew such actions to be wrong, and yet they destroyed people: this is frightening.

Second, although the prophets spoke in the name of the God of Israel, they did not hesitate to condemn the sins of those who claimed to follow the God of Israel. They unveiled the inhumanity of everyone they addressed, regardless of religion. If anything, they aimed their sharpest criticisms at the very people who professed allegiance to their God. The people who claimed to know the most religiously were held to a higher standard.

Regardless of our religious and cultural identities, these are convictions from the ancient prophets which should throb at the heart of the human rights movement: All cultures can commit atrocities; people generally know the difference between right and wrong, even while committing atrocities; religion does not always prevent human rights abuses.

2. The Jewish Diaspora in Exile

Not many people mention Shadrach, Meshach, and Abednego when discussing human rights. Who were these people? Why did Dr. King think this old story was so important for the civil rights movement?

These three bright Jewish young men appear in the Old Testament book of Daniel. They were taken as captives with Daniel from Jerusalem to Babylon in the sixth century BC and were trained as civil servants. Contrary to their captors' expectations, these young men maintained their Jewish identity, initially in a non-confrontational way. When their guard asked them to eat the rich food and wine of the palace, they did not reply, "Your food is an abomination to God;" they calmly asked permission to demonstrate that they would be healthier if they followed their Jewish food laws.

The relationship of the young men with the Babylonian state changed dramatically when King Nebuchadnezzar ordered all public servants to worship a newly erected idol. The three refused. Knowing they were at risk of death, they told the king, "Your Majesty, we will not serve your gods or worship the image of gold you have set up" (Daniel 3:18). This enraged Nebuchadnezzar, who threw them into a fiery furnace. To everyone's surprise, they survived.

As an historian of ethics, it interests me to see which dimensions of this story King did **not** use to explain his activism. King did not talk about the relations between minority and majority religions faced by his ancient heroes, though his minority African American Christianity had conflicts with the majority religions in America. King was gravely disappointed that white churches and synagogues did not rush to support the civil rights movement; nevertheless, King did not relate his three ancient Jewish heroes to the problems of relations between majority and minority religions.

It also interests me that King did not use the "beastly empire" theme to support his efforts. The account of his Jewish heroes is found in texts scholars call apocalyptic literature. In this literature several empires are described as devouring beasts, whether a lion, a bear, or a leopard, which destroy everything in their path. In view of the atrocities committed by the Assyrian and Babylonian Empires, such descriptions make sense. But Dr. King did not appropriate the beast theme for the civil rights movement; perhaps he had higher hopes for what would come from the American federal government.

Why did Dr. King cite Shadrach, Meshach, and Abednego? To legitimate carefully defined civil disobedience. For us in a post-Velvet Revolution society, it may be hard to grasp how deeply American civil rights leaders of the 1960s struggled to justify civil disobedience. They belonged to a community that viewed obeying the law as a binding moral obligation. An authoritative precedent was needed to modify this obligation. Following is a passage from the letter of April 12, 1963, signed by prominent Christian leaders and one rabbi from Birmingham, to which King was responding in his more famous letter:

"We clergymen are among those who, in January, issued 'an Appeal for Law and Order and Common Sense,' in dealing with racial problems in Alabama. We expressed understanding that honest convictions in racial matters could properly be pursued in the courts, but urged that decisions of those courts should in the meantime be peacefully obeyed . . . However, we are now confronted by a series of demonstrations by some of our Negro citizens, directed and led in part by outsiders. We recognize the natural impatience of people who feel their hopes are slow in being realized. But we are convinced that these demonstrations are unwise and untimely . . . We further strongly urge our own Negro community to withdraw support from these demonstrations."[16]

King penned his famous letter in response to this criticism while sitting in jail for leading a demonstration without a legal parade permit. According to the laws of the city of Birmingham, he was a criminal. Did his crime not discredit his cause and the entire civil rights movement? He answered that we are not morally obligated to obey unjust laws; indeed, sometimes we are morally required to disobey unjust laws.

"You express a great deal of anxiety over our willingness to break laws. This is certainly a legitimate concern. Since we so diligently urge people to obey the Supreme Court's decision of 1954 outlawing segregation in the public schools, it is rather strange and paradoxical to find us consciously breaking laws. One may well ask, 'How can you advocate breaking some laws and obeying others?' The answer is found in the fact that there are two types of laws: there are just laws, and there are unjust laws."

In this context he cites the example of Shadrach, Meshach, and Abednego. "There is nothing new about this kind of civil disobedience. It was seen sublimely in the refusal of Shadrach, Meshach, and Abednego to obey the laws of Nebuchadnezzar because a higher moral law was involved."

---

16   https://swap.stanford.edu/20141218230016/http:/mlk-kpp01.stanford.edu/king web/popular_requests/frequentdocs/clergy.pdf. Signed by C.C.J. Carpenter, D.D., LL.D., *Bishop of Alabama;* Joseph A. Durick, D.D., *Auxiliary Bishop, Diocese of Mobile-Birmingham;* Rabbi Milton L. Grafman, *Temple Emanu El, Birmingham, Alabama;* Bishop Paul Hardin, *Bishop of the Alabama-West Florida Conference of the Methodist Church;* Bishop Nolan B. Harmon, *Bishop of the North Alabama Conference of the Methodist Church;* George M. Murray, D.D., LL.D., *Bishop Coadjutor, Episcopal Diocese of Alabama;* Edward V. Ramage, *Moderator, Synod of the Alabama Presbyterian Church in the United States;* Earl Stallings, *Pastor, First Baptist Church, Birmingham, Alabama.*

These three are heroes precisely because they risked their lives to disobey an unjust law in order to obey a higher law. By citing these old names, King was not only defending his principles of non-violent civil disobedience; he was also challenging his Jewish, Protestant, and Catholic religious opponents to follow their own principles. He challenged them to find the religious courage to disobey unjust laws and follow a higher law as that law is found in their scriptures and in conscience. The civil disobedience of Shadrach, Meshach, and Abednego was sublime, making them King's ideal religious role models as defenders of human dignity.

3. Thomas Aquinas and the Higher Moral Law

Dr. King defended principled civil disobedience by citing his three Jewish heroes, but how can one distinguish between just and unjust laws? He continued to believe that obedience to just laws is morally required; morally legitimate civil disobedience requires a principled way to explain why and in what way a law is unjust. To address this question, King turned to the great Christian philosopher Thomas Aquinas (1225-1274). King wrote:

> "How does one determine when a law is just or unjust? A just law is a man-made code that squares with the moral law, or the law of God. An unjust law is a code that is out of harmony with the moral law. To put it in the terms of St. Thomas Aquinas, an unjust law is a human law that is not rooted in eternal and natural law. Any law that uplifts human personality is just. Any law that degrades human personality is unjust."

In his *Treatise on Law*,[17] Thomas Aquinas identified four types of laws: (1) the eternal law which exists in the reason or mind of God; (2) the natural law, which is the reflection or image of the eternal law within human reason by creation; (3) the divine law, which is the special revelation of God in the Bible; and (4) human laws, the fallible rules that are written and enforced in every society.[18] St. Thomas said that this last category, human law, could be just or unjust. "The ordinances human beings enact may be

---

[17] The following paragraphs about Thomas Aquinas are adapted from Thomas K. Johnson, *Human Rights: A Christian Primer*, 2nd ed., vol. 1, World Evangelical Alliance Global Issues Series (Bonn: VKW, 2016), 84, 85; available as a download here: https://www.academia.edu/36884876/Human_Rights_A_Christian_Primer.

[18] For more on how the theology and philosophy of law synthesized by St. Thomas can be appropriated within Protestant ethics, see Thomas K. Johnson, *Natural Law Ethics: An Evangelical Proposal* (Bonn: VKW, 2005), available as a download here: https://www.academia.edu/36884239/Natural_Law_Ethics_An_Evangelical_Proposal.

just or unjust. If they are just, then we have a moral obligation to obey them, since they ultimately derive from the eternal law of God . . . An ordinance may be unjust for one of two reasons: first, it may be contrary to the rights of humanity; and second, it may be contrary to the rights of God."[19]

Therefore, Aquinas concluded, we have no strict moral obligation to obey unjust laws, those laws which are contrary to human rights, though prudence calls for great caution before we disobey a human law. Moreover, in some situations people have a moral obligation to disobey an unjust law, which means engaging in civil disobedience. For King, following Aquinas, human rights activism requires determining when a law is so seriously unjust that responsible people should disobey an unjust law in order to obey a higher moral law.

Dr. King set his civil disobedience of the 1960s in the context of the heroes of Western civilization from the 1930s, 1940s, and 1950s, people who had disobeyed unjust human laws in order to obey higher laws. "We can never forget that everything Hitler did in Germany was 'legal' and everything the Hungarian freedom fighters did in Hungary was 'illegal.' It was 'illegal' to aid and comfort a Jew in Hitler's Germany. But I am sure that if I had lived in Germany during that time, I would have aided and comforted my Jewish brothers even though it was illegal. If I lived in a Communist country today where certain principles dear to the Christian faith are suppressed, I believe I would openly advocate disobeying these anti-religious laws." King believed his principles were the same as those of the anti-Nazi dissidents and of the anti-Communist dissidents.

This classical claim about civil disobedience, articulated by Aquinas and King, merits serious attention today. Responsible people must

---

[19]   Thomas Aquinas, Summa Theologica, question 96, article 4. The translation used is that of Manuel Velasquez (Copyright 1983), an excerpt of which appears in *Ethics: Theory and Practice*, edited by Manuel Velasquez and Cynthia Rostankowski (Prentice Hall, 1985), 41-54. The quotation is from pages 52 and 53. There are significant Latin-to-English translation questions regarding this text. Some translations use the term "human good" instead of "rights of humanity;" the term "rights of humanity" seems to fit the context better than does "human good." The choice Thomas made to locate his discussion of human rights within his discussion of the natural moral law indicates that he saw human rights protection as an organic part of the purpose of the natural moral law. Aquinas saw the natural law as God's universal moral law which is built into creation and into properly functioning practical reason. Because the natural moral law comes from God through creation, the content is consistent with the moral law specially revealed in the Bible. Regardless of the relation of people to the Bible, they receive great benefit from the natural moral law.

consider disobeying unjust human laws, precisely when those unjust laws are contrary to fundamental human rights. This approach does not make human laws appear to be of little importance. When a human law is just, claim Aquinas and King, all people have a God-given obligation to obey that law. The goal of civil disobedience must be to establish a just human law which protects human rights and is compatible with the higher moral law.

Dr. King did not quote unpronounceable ancient names when he mentioned the example of the early Christian church as a source of his civil disobedience on behalf of human rights. Nevertheless, the Christians of the first centuries were a source of powerful inspiration for King; his appeals to the early church were also a call for spiritual renewal in the churches of his time. He wrote, civil disobedience "was practiced superbly by the early Christians, who were willing to face hungry lions and the excruciating pain of chopping blocks before submitting to certain unjust laws of the Roman Empire." The role model, for King, was civil disobedience to the point of death because of one's religious and moral convictions. This willingness to suffer to the point of death was, in King's assessment, a source of tremendous spiritual power.

> "There was a time when the church was very powerful. It was during that period that the early Christians rejoiced when they were deemed worthy to suffer for what they believed. In those days the church was not merely a thermometer that recorded the ideas and principles of popular opinion; it was the thermostat that transformed the mores of society. Wherever the early Christians entered a town, the power structure got disturbed and immediately sought to convict them for being 'disturbers of the peace' and 'outside agitators.' But they went on with the conviction that they were a 'colony of heaven' and had to obey God rather than man. They were small in number but big in commitment . . . They brought an end to such ancient evils as infanticide and gladiatorial contest."

King thought that renewed churches in his time could bring an end to the evil of racial discrimination, but to do so they would need to risk facing hungry lions.

Conclusion

The human rights movement is delivering far less than was promised in 1948. That is why some serious souls, such as the commentator mentioned, are looking for new sources of courage and guidance in Martin Luther King, Jr. That is a good choice, since Dr. King and his principles brought vast changes in the United States and far beyond. But those principles are neither easy nor safe. Dr. King knew his principles would arouse powerful reactions and might lead to his death. Yet he exhorted his movement to risk death to overcome injustice.

To appropriate the perspective of Martin Luther King, one must not only read one or two of his texts or listen to some speeches. The direction suggested here is to also look to the sources used by Dr. King, such as the speeches of the prophets and the actions of Shadrach, Meshach, and Abednego. And to grasp justice, one must include a theory such as that of Thomas Aquinas; otherwise we easily confuse justice and injustice. But if one is willing to take those steps, one must be careful of what might follow.

Is Human Dignity Earned or Is Human Dignity a Gift?

A Contribution of the Evangelical Faith to Human Rights Discourse[20]

As we come to the end of the twentieth century, one of the greatest intellectual questions we face is "What is a human being?" In one way or another, this question is being discussed in many of the different academic disciplines: law, psychology, economics, sociology, art, philosophy, and theology. And the answers we find to this question are very important not only for our personal life but also for our life together in society, as neighbors. We need to understand the peculiar dignity and "humanness" of humanity, as we also need to understand the peculiar inhumanity of man to man.

In this essay I want to explore one small part of the question of human nature, namely, "Why is human life valuable?"—a question that can be made more pointed when phrased as, "Is human dignity earned or is human dignity a gift?" Differing views in this area lie immediately behind many of our other important questions, such as why we should protect human rights, why we should practice humanitarian aid and medical care, and why we should be concerned about the safety of the individual in daily life. And it is clear, I believe, that this is not only a question of metaethics; it is also a problem of basic philosophy. Any philosophy without a satisfactory explanation of the value of human life needs serious revision.

---

[20] This is a lightly revised version of a human rights lecture that Thomas K. Johnson originally delivered in May 1996 with the title "Why Is Human Life Valuable?" at a symposium of Russian- and English-speaking professors at the Livadia Palace in Yalta, Crimea — the palace where Stalin, Churchill, and Roosevelt met at the end of World War II. From 1994 to 1996 Johnson served as visiting professor of philosophy for the European Humanities University (EHU) in Minsk, Belarus. During this time he also gave guest lectures for various institutions in Belarus and Ukraine. EHU was started in 1992 as an openly pro-democracy university by scholars who had worked for the collapse of communism. It came into conflict with the Belarussian authorities as Belarus moved toward authoritarianism, starting in 1994. In 2004, the Belarussian government forced EHU to relocate to Lithuania because of its continued outspoken support of democracy. This essay was previously published by Martin Bucer Seminary as MBS Text 191 (2019), https://www.bucer.de/ressource/details/mbs-texte-191-2019-is-human-dignity-earned-or-is-human-dignity-a-gift.html.

In modern thought there tend to be two types of answers to why human life is valuable; some would claim that the dignity of the person is earned by some human function or ability while others claim that human dignity is a gift that is given in a relationship. The first approach can be called "functionalism," the second "personalism." Functionalist views of human value tend to arise within a naturalistic worldview. Personalist views of human dignity are usually found among theists. Functionalist views of human dignity sometimes lead to viewing *homo sapiens* who lack certain crucial functions as being sub-human and discardable. A personalist view of human dignity may lead us to significant sacrifices for our neighbors. This distinction between differing views requires explanation, first by illustrating functionalism, then personalism.

Functionalism

An interesting variety of functionalism is found in the writings of Michael Tooley, who inquired into "what properties a thing must possess in order to have a right to life."[21] Obviously a right to live is foundational for any other rights one might have. His answer goes something like this. He quotes Joel Feinberg: "The sorts of beings who can have rights are precisely those who have (or can have) interests." This means that "an entity cannot have any rights at all, and *a fortiori*, cannot have a right to life, unless it is capable of having interests."[22] And in order to have interests, it "must necessarily be a subject of conscious states, including experiences and desires."[23] And in order to have a desire for a continuing life, it must have a concept of a continuing self.

This all sounds eminently reasonable, but the problems become apparent once one sees how Tooley uses his principles. Obviously, he can defend abortion with this system. He also defends infanticide, because infants apparently do not have a concept of a continuing self. But many higher animals probably do have a right to live, presumably a right equal to that of human beings, because they seem to have an interest in and a concept of a continuing self. It is interesting that he uses the term "murder" to describe the killing of higher animals. And one is forced to suspect that a person in a short coma would not have any rights within his system of ethics. What

---

[21]   Michael Tooley, "In Defense of Abortion and Infanticide," in *Applying Ethics*, 4th edition, ed. Jeffrey Olen and Vincent Barry (Belmont, CA: Wadsworth Publishing Co., 1992), 176.

[22]   Tooley, 178.

[23]   Tooley, 181.

started as a theory of human rights leads to the conclusion that killing babies is morally acceptable, whereas eating meat or wearing leather shoes could be described as murder. This is a good indicator of the problem of starting with a human function, in this case having an interest, as the basis for the value of a person.

A somewhat similar variety of functionalism is found in the philosophy of Mary Anne Warren. She asks, "What sort of entity, exactly, has the inalienable rights to life, liberty, and the pursuit of happiness?"[24] Though she is obviously quoting the American Declaration of Independence (of 1776), her overall point of view is, I think, quite different from that of the Declaration. She suggests that we must make a distinction between genetic humanity and personhood, and that only persons, not genetic human beings, have moral rights. She says,

> "Imagine a space traveler who lands on an unknown planet and encounters a race of beings utterly unlike any he has ever seen or heard of. If he wants to be sure of behaving morally toward these beings, he has to somehow decide whether they are people, and hence have full moral rights, or whether they are the sort of thing which he need not feel guilty about treating as, for example, a source of food."[25]

In answering this question, Warren suggests that the traits of personhood are roughly the following:

1. consciousness, especially the capacity to feel pain,
2. reasoning,
3. self-motivated activity,
4. the capacity to communicate,
5. the presence of self-concepts and self-awareness.

Warren does not think an entity needs to meet all five criteria to be a person. The first two may be sufficient. But the absence of all five would surely indicate, she claims, that an entity is not a person and therefore has no moral rights.

Her list of traits of personhood has much value. These are, of course, traits we normally find in people. But the crucial question is whether one has to earn the status of personhood by means of having the normal

---

[24] Mary Anne Warren, "On the Moral and Legal Status of Abortion," in *Ethics: Theory and Practice*, ed. Manuel Velasquez and Cynthia Rostankowski (Englewood Cliffs, NJ: Prentice-Hall, Inc., 1985), 249.
[25] Warren, 250.

functions and abilities or if the status of personhood is given as a gift. Clearly her approach is a functionalist approach, and her answers will lead to the same problems as do Tooley's. She very candidly says that humans at the beginning and end of life may not be persons and that they are without moral rights.

A third good example of functionalism is found in the writings of process philosopher John B. Cobb, Jr. He claims that "although the right of a human being to life is quite fundamental, it is not absolute. It is derived from, and therefore subordinate to, the right of people to carry out their own projects."[26] Having projects to carry out is what gives distinctive value to human life and what confers rights on a person.

Cobb clarifies his view by way of two sharp contrasts. He contrasts the life of a person with the life of an infant and with the life of an animal. An infant on the way to personhood goes through two major transformations. The first is that while an infant lives fully in the present, a "child comes to have his or her own projects that demand respect."[27] The second is that in infancy, all experience is unified in serving the body, whereas a child uses the body to implement projects. And, Cobb believes, animals do not generally make the transition to using their bodies to fulfill projects beyond preservation of their bodies.

The problem with such a theory is that humans who do not yet or no longer have projects do not have the moral status of personhood, and therefore their lives have no particular moral value. On the other hand, some animals might cross the line to become persons. It is a clear example of functionalism, albeit with a distinctive perspective on what function is needed to earn human dignity.

These three examples are enough to illustrate that functionalism of one variety or another is widespread today. It is used to defend abortion, infanticide, active euthanasia, and animal rights. In every case, a person has to demonstrate certain abilities or functions in order to earn the status of personhood in the eyes of other people or of society at large. If one fails to earn the status of personhood, then one's life is not to be particularly protected morally or legally.

Obviously, all the philosophies mentioned represent Western individualism in some way. But a functional approach to the value of a person can easily be given a different ideological orientation. With the slightest bit of imagination, one can easily change which functions or abilities are needed

---

[26]   John B. Cobb, Jr., *Matters of Life and Death* (Louisville: Westminster John Knox Press, 1991), 74, 75.

[27]   Cobb, 83.

to earn "personhood." The functions selected can be economic, racial, religious, or related to one's value to the state. And then the definition of what makes human life valuable can be used to legitimate all sorts of atrocities, usually against some group of people not liked by the powerful. An analysis of the totalitarian ideologies of the people in the twentieth century who have committed the great crimes against humanity will yield a tragic set of variations on the same theme: personhood is something not all can earn. Functionalist ideologies have contributed to genocide and concentration camps. The philosophies of functionalism usually come with the high moral tone of explaining why human life is valuable, but they tend to end by explaining why the lives at the margins of some particular society are not to be valued. This calls into question the whole method and approach of functionalism.

Personalism

The alternate to functionalism is personalism. The belief that unites personalists, in the midst of very different ways of speaking, is that the value of human life is a gift, and the value of this gift is a "given" that is present even if particular human abilities or functions are missing. Generally, personalists think within the Judeo-Christian intellectual tradition and see their theories as an explanation of the biblical claim that human beings are created in the image of God.[28]

A prominent example of personalism in the political realm is the American Declaration of Independence. Warren failed to mention the part that says that all people are "endowed by their Creator" with unalienable rights. In eighteenth-century Anglo-American political discussions, some people said human rights were alienable, that they could be lost. This was one of the supposed moral defenses of slavery, and it bears a strong resemblance to functionalist views of human value. In conscious contrast to this, Thomas Jefferson and his colleagues claimed that human rights were inalienable because they were a gift from God.[29] In this way of thinking, the

---

[28] Irwyn Ince has argued that this biblical claim has always stood in tension with contrasting views of humanity. "In the ancient Near Eastern world, the *imago Dei* was a radically countercultural idea. The nations of that time recognized only one who imaged or embodied the gods, and that was the king. This image was not borne by the common person walking the street, and it certainly wasn't attributed to a woman." Irwyn Ince, Jr., *The Beautiful Community: Unity, Diversity, and the Church at its Best* (InterVarsity Press, 2020), 43.

[29] Several of the people who signed the American Declaration of Independence continued to own slaves even after they publicly affirmed ethical principles that

value of a person is not earned by any function or ability, and therefore the value of the person cannot be lost. To repeat the point, the dignity of a person is simply a gift from God.

A very different kind of personalism is found in the writings of Soren Kierkegaard (1813–1855), the nineteenth-century Danish philosopher often called the father of existentialism. In *Sickness unto Death* he writes,

> "The gradations in the consciousness of the self with which we have hitherto been employed are within the definition of the human self, or the self whose measure is man. But this self acquires a new quality or qualifications in the fact that it is the self directly in the sight of God. This self is no longer the merely human self but is what I would call, hoping not to be misunderstood, the theological self, the self directly in the sight of God. And what an infinite reality this self acquires by being before God! A herdsman who (if this were possible) is a self only in the sight of cows is a very low self, and so also is a ruler who is a self in the sight of slaves — for in both cases the scale or measure is lacking. The child who hitherto has had only the parents to measure itself by, becomes a self when he is a man by getting the state as a measure. But what an infinite accent falls upon the self by getting God as a measure."[30]

Kierkegaard claims that the value of the person is a relational notion, that value is given to the person by relations in which one stands. Then, if all people stand in some relation to God, whether conscious or unconscious, positive or negative, that relation gives infinite value to the person. Clearly this value is a gift independent of functions.

A great modern personalist was the German Evangelical theologian Helmut Thielicke (1908–1986), who wrote his treatises on ethics largely in reaction to the abuses of the Nazi era. He claimed that human dignity is always an *alien* dignity that comes as a gift from outside the self and not from any ontological qualities within the person, whether freedom, personality, responsibility, conscience, or any other capacity. His reason for thinking this was his claim that humans are relational entities, created in the image of God, created for a relationship with God. The image of God in man, he claims, does not have to do with attributes or properties of mankind. "It has reference rather to the alien dignity which man possesses by way of his divine prototype [*Urbild*], that original which is present in Christ

---

condemned slavery. This is a tragic example of the difference or even conflict between the professed beliefs and the practiced beliefs of a person or group of people.

[30]   Quoted by Helmut Thielicke, *Modern Faith and Thought*, trans. Geoffrey W. Bromiley (Grand Rapids: Eerdmans, 1990), 487.

alone."[31] When he uses the term "alien" to describe human dignity, he is consciously following Martin Luther's theology.

Luther said we cannot be acceptable to God on the basis of any inherent, internal goodness within ourselves, or on the basis of anything we do, but only on the basis of an alien, external righteousness credited to us as a gift in Christ. Thielicke claims that our dignity, like our righteousness, has to do with "God's remembrance of us,"[32] not with something internal within us. And because God remembers us, he speaks to us in creation and in Christ so that "The divine address constitutes the person."[33]

Even if a person is not aware of God, the fact that God has spoken to humanity constitutes the dignity of every person so that the dignity and value of each person is something that cannot be lost. Even if many normal human functions are lost, the value or dignity of the person is not lost, because it depends on God's remembrance of the person and God's speech to that person. And if human dignity is the result of God's speech to us, the fact of human dignity implies an important task, that of actualizing this relationship on the human side.[34]

Clearly, a personalist view of human value will lead to very different conclusions about many dimensions of contemporary life than will a functionalist view. Medical care, human rights, humanitarian aid, and personal safety are only a few of the areas that look different if seen through personalist eyes. And it should also be clear that functionalism is usually part of a materialist or naturalist worldview, while personalism is usually part of a theistic worldview. Although there may be atheistic personalists and perhaps also theistic functionalists, those combinations of beliefs would present severe internal contradictions.

It is often said that among Western intellectuals, belief in God died in the nineteenth century and belief in humanity died in the twentieth century. Contrary to the hopes of Friedrich Nietzsche (1844–1900), the death of belief in God did not lead us to become superior beings, or *Übermenschen* in his terminology; it led us to see each other as *Untermenschen*, as less than fully human. But as we now can clearly see both the cultural failure and the intellectual incoherence of atheistic naturalism, maybe we can hope that belief in both God and humanity can be recovered.

---

[31]   Helmut Thielicke, *Theological Ethics*, vol. 1, *Foundations*, trans. and ed. Wm. H. Lazareth (Grand Rapids: Eerdmans, 1979) 151, 152.
[32]   Thielicke, 165.
[33]   Thielicke, 164.
[34]   Thielicke, 158.

Unalienable Rights and Religious Freedom[35]

On July 8, 2019, the US State Department announced that it is forming a commission on unalienable human rights, presumably in relation to foreign policy, the realm of the State Department. This announcement has prompted a range of reactions. Some of the criticisms of the new commission were rather severe, hardly professional, raising an important question: Do the critics think the current administration can simply do nothing of value, or might the high school US government teachers of these critics not have risen to their jobs, leaving their students, the current critics, seriously deficient in their knowledge of American human rights principles?

One example of such criticism that seems to either arise from ill will or else is terribly uninformed is the July 18, 2019, letter of some 50 Democrat members of the US House of Representatives written to Secretary of State Mike Pompeo. The letter complains, "We require clear assurances that this Commission is not merely a scheme to inject religion into government policy-making. After all, the First Amendment guarantees the separation of church and state." This merits a response.

When we heard of the new commission, all politically educated Americans recognized that the term "unalienable rights" is a reference to the US Declaration of Independence of July 4, 1776. Since then, US spelling has changed; we have been saying "inalienable" for a long time. The "un" spelling sharpens the reference to the principles of 1776. There we find those memorable words:

> "We hold these truths to be self-evident, that all men are created equal, that they are endowed by their Creator with certain unalienable Rights, that among these are Life, Liberty and the pursuit of Happiness. That to secure these rights, Governments are instituted among Men, deriving their just powers from the consent of the governed, That whenever any Form of Government becomes destructive of these ends, it is the Right of the People to alter or to abolish it, and to institute new Government, laying its foundation on such principles and organizing its powers in such form, as to them shall seem most likely to effect their Safety and Happiness."

---

[35] This essay was initially published in *Providence*, August 8, 2019; https://providencemag.com/2019/08/unalienable-rights-and-religious-freedom/. Reprinted with permission.

What our high school government teachers should have taught us is that these words are heavily dependent on the Virginia Declaration of Rights, largely written by George Mason and published on June 12, 1776, some three weeks before the more famous Declaration of Independence. There we read:

> "That all men are by nature equally free and independent and have certain inherent rights, of which, when they enter into a state of society, they cannot, by any compact, deprive or divest their posterity; namely, the enjoyment of life and liberty, with the means of acquiring and possessing property, and pursuing and obtaining happiness and safety.
>
> That all power is vested in, and consequently derived from, the people; that magistrates are their trustees and servants and at all times amenable to them.
>
> That government is, or ought to be, instituted for the common benefit, protection, and security of the people, nation, or community; of all the various modes and forms of government, that is best which is capable of producing the greatest degree of happiness and safety and is most effectually secured against the danger of maladministration. And that, when any government shall be found inadequate or contrary to these purposes, a majority of the community has an indubitable, inalienable, and indefeasible right to reform, alter, or abolish it, in such manner as shall be judged most conducive to the public weal."

The famous words in the Declaration of Independence about unalienable rights are a shorter, more quotable version of the same ideas in the Virginia Declaration. But the Virginians explained unalienable rights more clearly. They are the rights that are inherent in a person and which cannot be given by a society nor taken away by a society. In this sense, they are natural rights, since they are given by nature, not given by society or government. These rights include the rights of life and liberty, to pursue property, happiness, and safety.

One point in which the Virginia Declaration differs from its famous younger sibling is how God is mentioned; this difference in the longer version should still the fears of those who ask if a new concern for unalienable rights endangers the separation of church and state. Whereas the theology of the Declaration of Independence describes God as the source of rights (people are "endowed by their Creator with certain unalienable Rights"), the Virginia text mentions God only in the paragraph regarding freedom of religion, section 16.

"That religion, or the duty which we owe to our Creator, and the manner of discharging it, can be directed only by reason and conviction, not by force or violence; and therefore all men are equally entitled to the free exercise of religion, according to the dictates of conscience; and that it is the mutual duty of all to practise Christian forbearance, love, and charity toward each other."

The main theological claim of the Virginia Declaration is that people are required to follow reason and conscience in the realm of religion in a manner that allows equal freedom to all people, specifically excluding the use of force or violence related to religion. This is the theological foundation for the separation of church and state written into the Bill of Rights a few years later. It came from representatives of the Virginia Enlightenment, some of whom were Christians, some Deists, and probably some who were undefined in their religion. If a few bore a grudge that there is reference to rational duties to our Creator, this must have been balanced by the duties to practice forbearance, love, and charity which are mentioned especially in relation to freedom of religion.

If the new commission advises the State Department regarding the principles implied by the use of the older terminology of "unalienable rights," not "inalienable rights," we should expect that State should emphasize those rights which are inherent in our humanness, such as life, liberty, and the freedoms of conscience, speech, and religion, along with the rights to pursue happiness, property, and safety. This terminology emphasizes that these rights are not given by society and may not be taken away by society or its government. They are dimensions of human dignity which governments exist to protect.

I asked if the critics of the new commission are so critical of the current administration that they believe nothing good can come from it, or if those critics are not familiar with American principles of human rights. It was a trick question; there is a third option.

Across the twentieth century, sometimes from totalitarian regimes, we heard the assumption that human rights come from the state or the governing party, that rights do not come from nature, God, or human dignity. I cannot evaluate the philosophical theories of fifty members of Congress and their staffs, but it would be terribly frightening if those fifty lawmakers believe they have the power to give human rights. What one can give one can also take away, including the rights of human beings. Such an assumption would make a branch of government a God-substitute, giving and taking rights, a denial of the declarations of 1776 and the Bill of Rights. Rather than properly separating church and state, such a theory of rights would put all our rights at risk.

We have a better option. Rather than endangering the separation of church and state, these classical American texts lay a firm foundation for human rights, including nuanced roles for church and state. Why not have a commission to reconsider "unalienable rights" and their application today? We might learn something!

Lessons from the Paris Attacks 2015

Clash of Civilizations or Battling Nihilisms?[36]

For about twenty years, because of important publications with similar titles from the pen of Samuel Huntington, it has been common to interpret international and cross-cultural events in light of "The Clash of Civilizations" theory. It was claimed that global and regional conflict would no longer be along ideological or economic lines, but rather between opposing civilizations. The several civilizations are distinguished from each other by language, history, culture, tradition, and, especially by different religions, with the role of religions in civilizations and inter-civilizational conflicts becoming increasingly large because of globalization. Some Christians liked the Huntington thesis because it recognized an important role of religions in society. But in recent times this theory has, in my opinion, been partly disproved because of the role that religious freedom can play in societies. Nevertheless, the clash of civilizations continues to have plausibility sufficient to influence both the interpretation of current events and the decisions of governments. I think this theory played a tragic role in shaping the American "War on Terror." And I heard this theory being used by some to interpret the tragic events in Paris over the last two weeks. As an alternative to the clash theory of civilizations, I would offer a different interpretation of what we saw in Paris. We should ask if we are seeing a cultural battle between different perceptions of nihilism, especially as different groups of people defend against the perceived nihilism of the other.

The word "nihilism" comes from the Greek word *nihil*, which means "nothing." One of the ways the word came into our modern languages was through the Judeo-Christian claim that creation is or was *ex nihilo*, meaning "from nothing." Those of us who studied Western civilization in American universities commonly associate nihilism with the name of Friedrich Nietzsche and his various intellectual heirs. Nietzsche and followers, or so we heard, believed in no objective truth, no objective right and wrong, no God's eye view of the universe. All we have, they claimed,

---

[36] This essay was first published by the World Reformed Fellowship on December 21, 2015, in light of the terrorist attacks in Paris on November 13, 2015, in which 130 people died, https://wrf.global/blog/blog-2/society/wrf-member-thomas-johnson-asks-about-lessons-paris-clash-civilizations-or-battling.

are competing examples of the will to power, with the important proviso that the elegant way to exercise the will to power is not by means of brutality but by means of telling a controlling narrative. By means of telling a compelling story, we create new values, even though no values exist outside the stories we tell.

Partly informed by such Nietzschean considerations, during the many years I taught university classes on the history of Western ethics, I often suggested that the era we call "modernity" was characterized by a significant shift in the way people in the West considered right and wrong. Prior to modernity, our Western cultural ancestors thought (at least those who were not nihilists) that right and wrong were somehow rooted in the nature of being or in the nature of the universe. This was true whether we studied Plato, the Stoics, the ancient Jewish philosophers such as Philo, or Christian thought from Augustine and Aquinas through Martin Luther and John Calvin. (It was even true of Aristotle and Old Testament books such as Genesis, Amos, and Proverbs.) A key phrase running through much of this moral/cultural heritage, especially during the fully developed stage of the biblical/classical synthesis, was "the natural law," meaning a moral law that was somehow related to that which truly is, to being itself. "Ought" was always based on "is;" "should" arose from the nature of being.

Starting with modernity, a huge change occurred across Western civilization, including both secularism and the Christian tradition, so that right and wrong were seen as based in history, not in being. We can take Thomas Hobbes's important book Leviathan, 1651, as a signal of the transition to modernity. At least as popularly understood, Hobbes taught that right and wrong are entirely rooted in the social contract by which society is formed. Outside the social contract, in the state of nature, there is only the war of all against all; within the social contract imposed by a sovereign on the people, there is the rule of law on the basis of which we know the difference between right and wrong. To note with especial clarity: within the modern Hobbesian worldview, it is not only our knowledge of right and wrong that is dependent on history; the very existence of right and wrong is dependent on historical facts, particularly whether or not a particular social contract exists. "Ought" was no longer based on "is;" ought was now seen as historically dependent or historically accidental. And after a study of Hobbes, my university students often seemed to feel threatened by nihilism, and during the classroom discussion they would begin grasping for some basis for morality or some explanation of right and wrong that was not entirely dependent on a particular political history which our neighbors might not share or accept.

It still surprises me (though I have known it for many years) that many religiously conservative Christians, many calling themselves pietistic, confessional, or evangelical, have been simultaneously partly modernist in their philosophy regarding the foundations of ethics. Even among Christians since Hobbes we find the new modernist idea that the existence of right and wrong, or our knowledge of right and wrong, is based entirely on particular historical facts. Specifically, many have thought, we would not know right and wrong if God had not given us the Bible or the Ten Commandments.

Please do not misunderstand me: I believe God gave us the Bible and that God placed the Ten Commandments with a special status within the Bible as written in stone. (I also read from both the Old and New Testaments in my quiet time this morning.) But prior to modernity, both Protestant and Catholic Christians generally said that God wrote his moral law on the human mind, heart, and conscience, as the image of his eternal moral character, as part of creation, which was repeated in the Ten Commandments. The pre-modern Christian view, taught by both Catholics and Protestants, was that both the existence of right and wrong and our knowledge of right and wrong were largely based on creation, not entirely on salvation history. But after Hobbes, many Christians started to sound a lot like Hobbes, saying that right and wrong are dependent on history and our knowledge of history, whether the history of a social contract (Hobbes) or the history of redemption recorded in the Bible (some Christians). Christians and secularists were too often united in separating ethics from being. This left Western culture sometimes fluctuating between feeling threatened by moral nihilism and accepting a historical moral authority that others perceived to be arbitrary.

I have been harsh in my description of my Christian community, so bear with my brief critique of Islam. It seems clear to me that many varieties of Islam had a weakness in the direction of the moral reasoning of modernity before the onset of modernity. Based merely on reading a few textbooks on Islamic history, theology, and ethics, it seems to me that Muslim ethics has frequently seen our knowledge of right and wrong as based entirely, or almost entirely, on history and our knowledge of that history. That is why the Koran and the early Muslim tradition play a different role in the life of the Muslim than I think the Bible should play in the life of a Christian. Well before the onset of modernity, Muslim theologians generally thought the proper knowledge of right and wrong was based on the Koran, the tradition, and the multiple schools of Islamic law, all of which are historically contingent. So far there has been very limited place for Muslim theologians to say that Allah wrote the demands of the Sharia onto the human heart, mind, and conscience in creation prior to giving the Koran, such that knowledge of the Sharia (and the difference between right and wrong) becomes partly independent from a particular historical community. Muslims may feel that any question about their prophet is blasphemous because it raises the specter of nihilism, the loss of all meaning and morals. At the same time, those of us who pointedly do not find our identity within Muslim history perceive the desired imposition of an ancient and harsh Sharia on our societies as either a power grab or an assault on all our meanings and morals, another specter of nihilism.

Seeing right and wrong, or our knowledge of right and wrong, as being entirely historically contingent truly does, I believe, leave us philosophically vulnerable to become nihilists. It is only a small step within the human mind from following modernity and saying my (or our) knowledge of right and wrong is entirely dependent on my history (whether as a Muslim, as a Christian, or as a follower of Hobbes) to feeling like a nihilist, that there are no universal moral rules that apply to all people everywhere. In my own study and university teaching, I always felt a steadily unfolding progression of ideas from Hobbes to Nietzsche. I am sure that basing ethics entirely on history (Hobbes) leads slowly but surely to nihilism, the loss of morals and meaning on the everyday level, as well as to the loss of ultimate truth claims. And we perceive this threatening nihilism more quickly among the people who do not share our own cultural or religious story. Muslims easily perceive both Christians and secularists as endangered by nihilism, and vice versa.

What we have seen recently on the streets of Paris is, I believe, the result of two battling nihilisms, more precisely, two groups of people striving to defend themselves against the threat of nihilism which they perceive in the historical relativism of their neighbors. They do not feel as if they can trust their neighbors to act on the basis of a standard of behavior which is suitable for all of humanity. By this I do not in any way imply a moral equivalency between the good work of the French police, defending their city and their citizens, and the truly evil work of terrorists murdering ordinary people. Nor do I imply that a handful of terrorists really represent many millions of Muslims. But I would call our attention to a philosophical similarity between radical Islam, admittedly more extreme than older Islam because of doctrinal changes, and Western democracy. Both separate knowledge of right and wrong from being; both say right and wrong are based on the way we tell the history of our community; both are left using force (one illegitimate, one legitimate) to enforce the values of their community without a satisfactory appeal to a non-historical basis for universal values or moral ideals; both feel like the other represents the threat of nihilism.

The gun battles in the Paris streets portray the conflict of competing nihilisms, Mohammed (as interpreted by extremists) versus Thomas Hobbes (as followed across modernity), unified in separating morality from the nature of being, but in such a way that most people perceive the implied nihilism in the worldview of the other before they perceive the threat of nihilism in their own worldviews. And we Christians often do not know what to say because we have neglected important themes in the classical Christian tradition of moral thought which connected ethics with being.

Obviously, I would like to see a renewed discussion of the relation between being and ethics, the natural moral law, in the spirit of the biblical/classical synthesis. This is essential to address the moral nihilism against which both radical Islam and Western democracies are fighting. As a small step in this direction, but with less metaphysics involved, I am sure there would be tremendous benefit in renewed global public discussion of the relation between universal human duties (with its own body of literature) and universal human rights (with a rich body of literature). Both of these discussions embody valuable ongoing echoes of the older tradition of discussing God's natural moral law. Both ongoing discussions represent models of the relation between particular religions and public life that avoid or reduce the threat of nihilism. Both discussions can be open to people of a variety of religions or of no defined religion in a manner that may help us to trust others to follow some defined standard of behavior. In my own writing I have attempted to contribute to both of these global discussions in a manner that is clearly rooted in my evangelical Christian convictions but is also open to discussion with people of other convictions.

The nihilism, more precisely the perceived threat of nihilism, embodied in the gunfire on the streets of Paris is, I think, more of a feeling than a reasoned package of convictions. Obviously, it has to be addressed by preachers and philosophers of religion as a fundamental human need to be addressed by faith. But nihilism is not only a faith problem; good moral reason also has a role to play. We can have more public considerations of universal human rights and universal human duties, along with the religious and philosophical discussion of what those duties/rights are and where they originate, so the relation between ethics and being as least gets back on the table.

The problem in Paris goes beyond gathering intelligence about future terrorists or better efforts to integrate religious minorities and immigrants into Western democracies, though those steps are essential. The problems illustrated on the streets of Paris are also problems of fundamental moral philosophy. Are there reasons not to be nihilists that are not only based in my telling of my community's story, reasons that I can explain to people who follow another story or religion? That is part of the challenge for Christian moral philosophers today.

Religious Terrorism, Brussels, and the Search for Meaning[37]

After the recent terrorist attacks in Brussels, news reporters are again rais-ing the agonizing question of why so many young people who have grown up in Europe are being radicalized and joining ISIS or other extremist reli-gious organizations. The statistics are truly disturbing. One reporter claims Belgians are joining extremist organizations at a rate of almost 42 per million, so that over 500 Belgians have joined violent extremist organ-izations from a population of only about 11.2 million.[38] In contrast, a dip-lomat from Indonesia is very happy that only a few hundred of his fellow citizens, a population of some 200 million, of whom 87% are Muslims, have deserted their communities to fight for the Islamic State and its allies.[39] If Indonesians went to fight for ISIS at rates similar to Belgians, there should be over 8,000 Indonesians in the ISIS armies. But why are so many Europe-ans joining ISIS?

There is, rather obviously, significant religious, cultural, relational, and ethical content that lies upstream from the decisions of the many young European Muslims who join extremist organizations. Some of that content is likely to be found in immediate personal or family matters, whether a conflict within the family, a romance gone sour, or a fight at school. And the lack of education, good jobs, and full acceptance of Muslims in Europe surely plays an important role. If young men are fully engaged in develop-ing careers, romance, friends, and families, and feel esteemed as good Eu-ropeans while doing so, they will have something they do not want to leave behind to become suicide bombers. However, the largely secularized char-acter of our education, as Western observers, may blind us, so we do not

---

[37] This was first published by the World Reformed Fellowship on March 29, 2016. On March 22, 2016, there were three coordinated terrorist attacks in Brussels which killed 35 people and injured about 300, https://wrf.global/blog/blog-2/current-issues-2/wrf-member-dr-thomas-johnson-writes-prague-about-religious-terrorism-brussels-and.

[38] https://pietervanostaeyen.wordpress.com/2016/02/02/february-2016-a-new-sta-tistical-update-on-belgian-fighters-in-syria-and-iraq/

[39] Prof. Agdurrahman Mas'ud, General Director of the Ministry of Religious Affairs of the Republic of Indonesia, in a public discussion in Brussels on March 19, 2015, held jointly by the Robert Schuman Foundation, the Forum Brussels International, and the Hanns Seidel Foundation. See Bonn Profiles 347, https://www.bucer.de/ressource/details/bonner-querschnitte-112015-ausgabe-347-eng.html.

perceive a crucial dimension of the complex phenomenon of religious extremism. It would be a mistake to only perceive the social/economic roots of religious extremism and terrorism. To grasp a depth dimension of the problem, I believe we should apply the observations of Holocaust survivor Viktor Frankl articulated in his powerful book from two generations ago, *Man's Search for Meaning*.[40]

Frankl, who was an Austrian Jew trained as a psychiatrist, noticed in some detail who, from among his fellow prisoners in a Nazi concentration camp, survived the ordeal, even though the harsh conditions should probably have killed them. His answer was that those prisoners who found meaning in life often survived the Holocaust under conditions that should have killed them, while those who lost any meaning usually died. Meaning was a source of life. This is a foundational observation about human life that should inform our considerations of religiously motivated violence and extremism.

I wish Frankl had more strongly emphasized that meaning, a source of life, can also become a source of death. Think of the National Socialist political and military machine that was itself a gigantic collectivist search for meaning filled with quasi-religious slogans, symbols, and mythology. One of my colleagues describes the Nazi movement as a "War Religion."[41] Maybe we could call National Socialism a "Death Religion." The Nazis found meaning in life in the wrong way. Appropriate meanings support life and keep people alive through circumstances that should have killed them; inappropriate meanings lead to death and the destruction of entire societies. We humans simply cannot avoid the search for meaning, whether it turns us into saints or demons.

This should inform our responses to the Islamic State's global recruiting efforts. It is not only a lack of social integration, education, and jobs that drives young Muslims into the arms of ISIS; it is also a quest for meaning. And the promise of a caliphate fills this meaning vacuum in a truly *dramatic* manner. It fills their hearts! Meaninglessness and *anomie* are gone forever! They have a purpose in life! What could be more spiritually and morally satisfying! (I suppose convinced Nazis had a similar experience.) And, therefore, if we want to truly reduce the attractiveness of ISIS in a serious manner, we simply must address the meaning question, however difficult it will be. And addressing the meaning question in

---

[40]   Viktor E. Frankl, *Man's Search for Meaning,* first English translation under the title *From Death-Camp to Existentialism,* 1959, first published in German in 1946. Various editions are now available in English.

[41]   Thomas Schirrmacher, *Hitlers Kriegsreligion,* 2 vol. (Bonn: VKW, 2007).

relation to ISIS throws us into the confused border zones between public ideology and religion.

Most of us who have read even one news report about ISIS have immediately noticed that at the center of the problem lies the relation between a religion and a state or a state-like entity. If ISIS were only a religious movement that invited people to become members, such that it did not have a state-like entity (including military force) controlled by its ideology, it would no longer be so very threatening. Indeed, the attractiveness of ISIS as a meaning-providing movement comes, in part, from the way in which it combines an ideology for shaping the public life of a state with a radical type of religion. But how can we respond to the overpowering quest for meaning without confusing the type of ideology needed for shaping a state with those deep human needs which are purely religious? How do we respond to the quest for meaning without ourselves confusing the need of a state for an official ideology and the need of most humans for a religion? Can we respond to the need for meaning without confusing religion and the realm of the state?

The solution, I believe, is that we truly must clarify the types of meanings related to faith communities and the types of meanings related to civil communities, as well as how faith and reason have different relations to the meaning of life in both faith and civil communities. I will use myself as an example. I am a Christian apologist who argues that the ultimate meaning of life is properly found in dialogue with the God of the Bible, the central theme in Christian churches; I am also a social philosopher who argues that there are multiple secondary meanings that are properly practiced and communicated in our multiple civil communities. And a proper relation between ultimate meaning and secondary meanings in life is crucial to overcoming religious extremism (the immediate background for religious terrorism), regardless of the faith community to which one belongs.

In our civil communities, such as stores, schools, hospitals, banks, factories, sports teams, research institutes, media outlets, government agencies, and humanitarian aid organizations, we should both practice and teach important secondary meanings. These secondary meanings include practicing justice, honesty, diligence, loyalty, and mercy, while talking about both universal human dignity and universal duties. These secondary meanings are real and address, in part, the human search for meaning, while directing the ultimate level of the search for meaning in a constructive direction. Religious extremism is, I believe, a response to a perceived meaning deficit in our multiple civil communities; the religious extremist perceives civil communities as not being filled with values and, therefore, as valueless. Pure secularism not only empties the heavens of ultimate meaning; pure secularism can easily empty all of life of meaning, including the life of our civil communities, furthering the meaning deficit that invites an extremist response. But this deficit of meaning can be addressed in ways that do not destroy the needed boundaries regarding church/state relations, though it will require much careful effort.

In the Western world we have spent centuries of blood, sweat, and tears to develop somewhat peaceful patterns of church/state relations, but it would be a terrible tragedy if we interpret these church/state relations in such a manner that we empty life in our civil communities of ethical meaning. The loss of ethical meaning in our civil communities feeds religious extremism. People will search for meaning, sometimes leading to life, sometimes leading to death, so that the quest for meaning is not only a private, personal matter. The lack of meaning has consequences for entire societies.

Obviously, addressing the need for meaning is a central task of faith communities, but within faith communities, to the extent of my experience and observation, the emphasis naturally falls on ultimate meanings. Within Christian churches we talk constantly about the hope of eternal life, about grace and forgiveness, about faith in the gospel. Within churches we sometimes talk about how God's grace should equip us to become salt and light within the civil communities, but, honestly, we must improve both our talk and our walk in this area. We can do better, in words and in practice, in our efforts to demonstrate how the ultimate meaning found in dialogue with God bears fruit in the secondary meanings appropriate to the civil communities. I think other faith communities face a similar problem, and this is more extremely true of those religious communities which turn in an extremist direction.

To avoid misunderstanding, I should say that in the part of the Christian community in which I live, ultimate meanings and faith are not seen as a leap into a realm of irrationality, such that ultimate meanings are irrational and secondary meanings are rational. Once again on Easter I heard that there are rational reasons to believe in the resurrection of Jesus. But there is a difference in the relation between faith and reason, depending on whether we are talking about ultimate or secondary meanings. In the realm of ultimate meanings, I believe it is far better for all of us (regardless of faith community) if we do not completely leave rationality behind. And in the realm of secondary meanings, when we are talking about ethical principles that should provide meaning to civil communities, it is simply foolish if we pretend to leave our respective faith identities behind. Our use of reason to articulate ethical meaning in the civil realms is always influenced by our faith identity, whether Christian, Jewish, Muslim, Atheist, Hindu, or Buddhist.

Nevertheless, there is an important difference in the relation between faith and reason, depending on whether we are discussing ultimate meanings in faith communities or secondary meanings in civil communities. In a faith community, it is far better if we never forget rationality while discussing ultimate meanings; in our civil communities, we should not forget the role of faith while using reason to articulate secondary meanings. But it will continue to be self-destructive if Western society does not use reason to articulate secondary meanings, the ethical principles needed for the healthy life of civil communities, most of which (both secondary meanings and civil communities) we share with people from many faith communities. (In Christian theological language, such a use of moral reason is possible because God's natural moral law provides the necessary pre-condition for moral reason, even though sin tends to make us misuse or misinterpret God's natural moral law.) We must fully engage our minds and the best ethical reasoning we have at our disposal to articulate and apply the moral meanings of all our civil communities.

At this point in history, I believe our two greatest dangers are either that we neglect the need for meaning as a background cause for the attractiveness of religious extremism or that we neglect the need to articulate authentic secondary meanings within our civil communities. We must respond, using our roles within both our faith communities and our civil communities. Religious extremism cannot be fully addressed by acting as if man can live from bread alone, without addressing the deeper human needs that lead to extremism, and these needs include the search for meaning. But we must not only address the need for ultimate, religious meaning; we must also address the need for secondary meanings in our civil communities. Otherwise we will hardly touch the existential needs being addressed by ISIS and similar movements. And unless our response to religious extremism includes religious, moral, and ideological responses, it will be very difficult to defeat.

Do Human Rights Need Christian Ethics?[42]

In spite of the growth of democracy in much of the world, there is still reason to be very concerned about the protection of human rights. In addition to the terrorism associated with matters in the Middle East, the genocide associated with conflicts in Africa, the seemingly growing religious persecution in several parts of the world, and widespread abortion in much of the first and second worlds, two particular matters merit our attention, since they represent similar events in several parts of the world. The first of these: the European Humanities University of Minsk, Belarus, a fine liberal arts university with an openly pro-democracy orientation, was closed by force at the orders of the dictator in 2004 as part of a general crackdown on any persons or groups seeking political, economic, or religious freedom. This was a clear violation of freedom of speech which should provoke indignation among all people of good will. Much to our regret, totalitarianism is not dead in the post-communist world.

A second matter that should provoke our concern is the loss of civil rights due to the expanding influence of certain types of Islam. It is noteworthy that the Dutch press, made sensitive to these matters by recent events in the Netherlands, is taking a serious interest in the new use of Islamic Shariah law in Ontario, Canada. Women from Iran, who fled to Canada to find equal protection for the rights of women, are now terrified that their rights will be abused by the imposition of the Shariah within a Western democracy. As one Muslim spokeswoman in Ontario put it, "Women and children are being sacrificed on the altar of multiculturalism."[43] If multiculturalism means that all systems of law, including those that do not

---

[42] Much of the content of this article was first presented as a special lecture at the European Humanities University in Minsk, Belarus, in 1996. This article is written in honor of my brave colleagues from EHU who have struggled to gain protection for basic rights in the face of grave personal danger. It was my privilege to serve with them as a Visiting Professor of Philosophy for five semesters, February 1994 through June 1996. An earlier version of this article was published as "Human Rights and Christian Ethics" in the theological journal of the Protestant Theological Faculty of Charles University in Prague, *Communio Viatorum* Volume 2005, XLVII, Nr. 3, 325-334, and also by Martin Bucer Seminary as MBS Text 54 (2005), https://www.bucer.de/ressource/details/mbs-texte-054-2005-human-rights-and-christian-ethics.html.

[43] Quotation from Alia Hogben in "Moslimvrouwen en Canada vrezen shariarechtbank" (translation of title: "Muslim women in Canada are afraid of Sharia courts") by Marjon Bolwijn in *de Volkskrant,* June 15, 2005, p. 4.

protect human rights, are now acceptable in the West, the rights of more people will be at serious risk, even within our Western democracies that claim to stand under the rule of law.

Heart-rending problems such as these will not be eliminated merely by philosophical clarity on the theory of rights, but the practical problems may be compounded by the widespread confusion on the topic of human rights found in the writings of many ethicists and philosophers today. And just as the concern to protect human rights arose largely under the influence of the Christian movement, it may be possible for a clear theory of rights to arise in the Christian community and then cross over into the broader political culture.[44]

One of the earlier Christian ethicists to write on the topic of human rights was Thomas Aquinas (1225–1274). Though what he wrote on the topic was brief, his incisive analysis provides a very constructive starting point that can be easily clarified and expanded by bringing it into dialog with recent theories and questions. St. Thomas asks, "Are we morally obligated to obey human laws?" His question assumes his distinctions between the four types of laws: (1) the eternal law which exists in the reason or mind of God; (2) the natural law, which is the reflection or image of the eternal law written by creation into human reason; (3) the divine law, which is the special revelation of God in the Bible; and (4) human laws, the very fallible rules written and enforced in every society. The answer Thomas gives to his own question is very interesting.

> "The ordinances human beings enact may be just or unjust. If they are just, then we have a moral obligation to obey them, since they ultimately derive from the eternal law of God . . . An ordinance may be unjust for one of two reasons: first, it may be contrary to the rights of humanity; and second, it may be contrary to the rights of God."[45]

---

[44] Some of this history is told by Max L. Stackhouse in *Creeds, Society, and Human Rights: A Study in Three Cultures* (Grand Rapids: Eerdmans, 1984), especially chapters two and three. A concern to protect human rights within secular society should probably be seen as a result of God's common or civilizing grace, which must be clearly distinguished from God's saving or special grace in Christ. As has often been mentioned by theologians studying God's common grace, there is some type of cooperation between common grace and special grace, since there is a unity within the eternal plan of God. Such common, civilizing grace has allowed many moral beliefs and theories to arise within the Christian community and then find further reception and application in wider circles of political culture. See especially J. Douma, *Algemene Genade: Uiteenzetting, vergelijking en beoordeling van de opvattingen van A. Kuyper, K. Schilder en Joh. Calvijn over "algemene genade"* (Goes: Oosterbaan & Le Cointre B. V., 1981).

[45] Thomas Aquinas, *Summa Theologica*, question 96, article 4.

The conclusion that Aquinas draws from this assessment is that people have no strict moral obligation to obey unjust laws, though prudence does require great caution before deciding to disobey a law. However, in some situations, one may have a moral obligation to disobey a seriously unjust law, which is to practice civil disobedience.

1. The Proper Function of Human Rights Claims

This assessment of Aquinas gives us the classical Christian definition of the proper function of human rights claims: to show that the actions of a government are so terribly unjust that one should protest or disobey. There are several ideas related to this definition of the function of human rights claims that Aquinas either assumes or articulates. He assumes that the proper function of government is to protect human rights by means of enforcing just laws. He clearly teaches that there is a standard of justice higher than government, a standard which exists in the eternal mind of God. He believes that human beings have rights because they are created in the image of God. And he argues that human practical reason, the image of God's reason, can generally, with careful use, write laws that are more just than the laws of his day.

The importance of this classical Christian theory of human rights became much clearer during the course of the twentieth century, and that for a profound but simple reason. During the twentieth century many of the worst crimes against humanity were committed by several governments against their own citizens or against people over whom they ruled. One can easily mention the Nazi Holocaust, the Stalin purges and death camps, the atrocities in Asia during World War II, South African Apartheid, and many other events that properly belong in a nightmare. At the time when people often looked to government to protect them, they mostly needed protection from an unjust government, often from their own government. One can see why the Apocalypse of John portrays unjust government as a devouring beast. Helmut Thielicke sagely commented, "Man must be protected against himself. The so-called basic rights, or human rights, have been formulated in light of this insight. From the dawn of their first realization they contain a protest against the trend of the state towards omnipotence."[46]

---

[46]   Helmut Thielicke, *Theological Ethics*, vol 2: *Politics*, edited and translated by William H. Lazareth (Grand Rapids: Eerdmans, 1979), 230, 231.

2. The Ontological Status of Human Rights Claims

Unfortunately, the classical Christian philosophy of rights has been widely denied in philosophy in the twentieth century. One can understand this problem by asking ontological questions such as "Do human rights really exist?" and "What is the source of human rights?" The answers one en-counters to such questions are quite disturbing when viewed from within the classical Christian perspective. For example, Delos McKown writes, "The concept of inherent, natural human rights was at best a useful myth in the days of yore, but it was a myth nevertheless, with all the vulnerabil-ity that this implies. Accordingly, the idea of natural human rights should be demythologized."[47] If human rights are seen as a myth to be demythol-ogized, our culture has truly fallen into metaphysical despair, without a theoretical foundation for government or justice.

There are three types of answers to the question "Where do rights come from?" The first says that human rights come from the state or from society. Variations on this theme are found both in Western democratic philosophy and in Marxist or Communist philosophy. For example, Soviet Secretary Leonid Brezhnev, without doubt following the official com-munist line of thought, wrote, "The rights and freedoms of citizens cannot and must not be used against our social system," clearly assuming that rights come from the government or the communist party.[48] Strangely, this is not very different from what one finds in the works of some Western humanists. For example, Paul Kurtz wrote, "Rights have evolved out of the cultural, economic, political, and social structures that have prevailed."[49] In other words, rights come from society and/or government. The obvious problem with any theory that says that rights come society or the state is that what the state gives the state can take, leaving people with the im-pression that they are the property of the state and without an effective way of talking about the fundamental injustice of many states. If one says rights come from the state or from society, the discussion of human rights has lost its fundamental purpose and function.

The second answer to where human rights come from is to say that rights come from the self. This is most commonly found in Western liber-alism. A typical representative philosopher, Michael Tooley, claims that rights are based on the interests of the individual and that the interests of

---

[47]   As quoted in David A. Noebel, *Understanding the Times* (Summit Press, 1991), 512.
[48]   As quoted in Noebel, 533.
[49]   Paul Kurtz, *Forbidden Fruit* (Buffalo: Prometheus Books, 1988), 196. Quoted in Noe-bel, 510.

the individual are based on the consciousness and desires of that individual.[50] This type of individualism can be seen as the extreme opposite of the collectivism that says rights come from the state or from society. It too has serious philosophical problems. On the one hand, it leads to unlimited and irrational claims of rights, for once I say my rights come from my interests and desires, it is difficult to say which interests and desires do not lead to rights. Maybe I have a right to everything I desire. On the other hand, if I have no desires or interests, maybe I have no rights at all. This is why Western liberalism cannot decide if I have unlimited rights or no rights.

In passing, one should notice two serious problems that arise whether one claims rights come from the self or one claims rights come from the state/society. The first can be called "functional dehumanization." Both collectivism and individualism strongly tend to see the value of a person as rooted in some function or ability. Western liberal individualism tends to see the value of the person as rooted in a function such as the ability to communicate, the ability to reason, or the ability to be creative. Collectivist theories tend to see the value of the person as rooted in a societal function, such as the ability to be economically productive or to contribute to a particular type of society. The similarity between the two is that the value of the person is based in some function or ability. Rather consistently, both individualism and collectivism tend to think that a person who has lost or has never had some particular function or ability is sub-human or a non-person, and therefore without all rights. People without the ability to function in a particular way, as defined within the theory ruling over that society, are then discarded, whether through a concentration camp, abortion, euthanasia, or some other means.

The second serious problem that arises from both individualist and collectivist theories of the origin or source of human rights is that human rights are seen as alienable. This is closely related to the problem of functional dehumanization. When the American Declaration of Independence claimed that people are endowed by their Creator with unalienable rights, a very important claim was being made. This is that certain basic rights cannot be lost, whereas rights that are alienable can be lost or given away. In some varieties of seventeenth- and eighteenth-century philosophy, the individual was seen as the source and owner of rights, but these rights could be given away in exchange for security, since the rights were alienable. Once these rights were given away to the sovereign, or so it was claimed, the individual no longer had any rights over against the sovereign

---

[50]   See Michael Tooley, "In Defense of Abortion and Infanticide," in *Applying Ethics*, edited by Jeffrey Olen & Vincent Barry, (Wordsworth, 1992), 176–185.

state, which began to lay the theoretical foundation for totalitarianism.[51] This made the claim that some rights are unalienable very important.

The third type of answer to the question of the source of human rights is to say that rights come from God. This is, of course, the classical Christian point of view seen in the great Christian thinkers, based on the biblical account of humans being created in the image of God. This point of view is also seen, more or less, in many of the deist thinkers of the Enlightenment, who tended to selectively accept some ideas from classical Christianity, insofar as they related to political ethics.[52] This point of view claims that human rights come from God without regard to functions or abilities a person may or may not have, and that some basic rights cannot be taken away by the state or society. There is, thus, an ultimate guarantee of the value of each human life, such that an attack on a person is ultimately an attack on God.

It is best to interpret the classical Christian understanding of the value of human life as a gift that comes from God that is therefore extrinsic to the person and not to talk as if humans have some inherent or intrinsic dignity or value. Helmut Thielicke coined the term "alien dignity" to describe how Christians should see the value of each human life.[53] Contained within this term is a reference to the classical Reformation theology of salvation that used the term "alien righteousness;" this term means that Christ's righteousness is accounted to the believer as a gift that comes from outside the person and is, in a sense, alien to a person's status as a sinner. In an analogous manner we see the dignity of each person as a gift that comes to each person because of how God sees that person.

History would indicate that one does not necessarily need to be an orthodox Christian to say that human rights come from God, even though the belief in the dignity and value of a person that comes to political expression in the discussion of human rights is rooted in the biblical belief system. The choice of Thomas Aquinas to include his discussion of human rights within his discussion of the natural moral law is an indication of his intuition that the awareness of the value and rights of people is rooted in God-given practical reason as well as being rooted in the biblical account of creation. The awareness of the value and rights of humans given in

---

[51] The classical representative of this point of view is Thomas Hobbes, *Leviathan* (1651). In his philosophy, human rights arise from the self and are transferred to the Sovereign, showing that individualism and collectivism are not truly polar opposites, as is usually claimed.
[52] Good examples would be the political philosophy of John Locke and Thomas Jefferson, which led to the American Declaration of Independence.
[53] Helmut Thielicke, *Politics*, 305 and 393; also, elsewhere throughout his works.

nature (regardless of the religions of the people involved) is strengthened and renewed by the deeper awareness of the value and rights of humans given by grace in special revelation and redemption, known by faith in Christ. For this reason, it is possible for the perception of and concern for human rights to flow out from the believing community into the secular community; people of any faith or none, according to Aquinas, should know something about human dignity and the proper ways of treating other people. Nevertheless, the full explanation of the value and rights of men and women is given only in the biblical account of creation. If Western culture is in a status of metaphysical despair, without an account of human dignity, value, and rights, the time may be ripe for a theory of human rights firmly rooted in classical Christian thought to flow into the broader stream of Western culture.

3. What Rights Do People Truly Have?

The discussion of human rights starts to become much more specific when one asks what rights people have. The answers one hears about what rights people have seem to be partly dependent on one's theory about the origin of those rights. Thus, writers who think that rights come from the state or from society will be inclined to think people have whatever rights the state or society provides, which tends to lead to very short, limited lists of human rights. And writers who claim that rights come from the self tend to write as if we have as many rights as we want, which tends to lead to wildly exaggerated lists of supposed rights that may resemble a child's Christmas wish list. These opposing tendencies may make particular human rights claims sound arbitrary and therefore not worthy of serious consideration.

As an example of this problem one can look at the United Nations' Universal Declaration of Human Rights. Parts of this document are worthy of the most serious consideration. Article 4 claims, "No one shall be held in slavery or servitude; slavery and the slave trade shall be prohibited in all their forms." One can seriously hope that people of good will say, "Of course." But article 25 claims, "Everyone has the right to a standard of living adequate for the health and well-being of himself and of his family, including food, clothing, housing and medical care and necessary social services, and the right to security in the event of unemployment, sickness, disability, widowhood, old age or other lack of livelihood in circumstances beyond his control." Statements like article 25 may easily discredit most claims to violations of human rights, for suddenly it sounds like there is a moral equivalency between a government not providing very high unemployment benefits and a government selling people (or allowing people to be sold) into slavery. Article 25 sounds like a responsible wish list for a humane society, but it seems to be associated with the assumption that we have as many rights as we want, because rights come from the self. It bears repeating that such over-extended claims to seemingly unlimited rights can easily discredit the entire effort to consider human rights seriously.

A good way to begin considering what rights people have is to go back to the view of the person in classical Christian natural law theory, in which classical human rights theory is rooted. Thomas Aquinas and the other classical Christian philosophers saw the person as naturally living with a number of moral obligations which are rooted in the requirements of practical reason and everyday life. From this one can easily conclude that people have rights to do the things they are morally obligated to do. Our rights correspond with our moral duties.

Specifically, people feel a moral obligation, for example, to speak, worship, assemble, work, raise a family, and educate their children, leading to rights to do these things. These matters could be designated our "primary positive rights." In order to protect such primary rights, we need to have some specific legal arrangements and principles, matters such as fair trials and the principle that one is "innocent until proven guilty." These could be called procedural rights that protect primary and basic rights. And the term "basic rights" could be used to designate those things that are presupposed in our moral obligations, matters such as rights to life, liberty, and the pursuit of happiness. Obviously, basic rights must be protected in order to allow people to exercise their primary positive rights.

Some further illustrations may be in order. In the realm of work, the result of this type of human rights theory would be the following: Obviously a wise government will follow well- considered economic policies that promote the availability of good jobs, but there is no fundamental injustice, no violation of human rights, unless government interferes with a person's moral obligation to work. In the realm of education: Obviously, a stable government and healthy economy require a well-educated population, so the government has a legitimate interest in both elementary and higher education. But individuals, families, and local communities feel strong obligations to speak their mind, practice their religion, and educate their children in light of their own convictions and beliefs. Thus, there is a violation of human rights if any government carries out its proper obligations in a manner that prevents individuals and families from carrying out their moral obligations.

Observations

This general approach to human rights theory is clearly rooted in Christian ethics; however, it is a set of ideas that could probably be appropriated by people who may not share those Christian beliefs. It is possible that this way of talking about human rights could cross over from the Christian community into our wider political culture and provide additional clarity about one of the fundamental problems of politics.

Is Secularism the Primary Source of Religious Freedom?[54]

A Christian Response

Two truths should shape our discussions of religion and public life. First: religious persecution not only hurts or kills individuals and decimates religious communities; the lack of religious freedom contributes to many social problems, whereas freedom of religion contributes immensely to the well-being of society.[55] This is well-documented social science. Second: the repression of religious freedom is extremely high today, seemingly much higher than in the past. And the problem is almost certainly rising.[56] From these two truths arises a crucial question: why are there exceptions? Why do some people enjoy high levels of freedom of religion for generations? My great grandparents, grandparents, parents, children, and grandchildren have had the extraordinary privilege of living in one of those small pockets in the world which enjoy freedom of religion. Why do those pockets exist? What can be done to expand them? What cultural belief systems create and protect religious freedom?

One commonly hears that freedom of religion in the West arose out of a compromise between religions and secularism, such that secularism is seen as the source and guarantor of religious freedom.[57] But this

---

[54] This paper is an edited version of a speech given at the International Consultation on Religious Freedom held by the International Institute for Religious Freedom (WEA) in Istanbul, Turkey, March 16-18, 2013. It was first published as "Religious Freedom and the Twofold Work of God in the World," in the *International Journal for Religious Freedom*, Vol 6:1/2 2013. IJRF is available as a free download at https://www.iirf.eu/.

[55] See Brian J. Grim, "Religious Freedom and Social Well-being: A Critical Appraisal," IJRF Vol. 2:1, 2009, 37-46; see also Timothy Samuel Shah, principal author; Matthew J. Franck, editor-in-chief; and Thomas F. Farr, chairman of The Witherspoon Task Force on International Religious Freedom, with contributions by David Novak, Nicholas Wolterstorff, and Abdullah Saeed, *Religious Freedom: Why Now? Defending an Embattled Human Right* (Princeton, New Jersey, USA: The Witherspoon Institute, Inc. 2012).

[56] See Brian J. Grim, "Rising Restrictions on Religion: Context, Statistics, and Implications," IJRF Vol. 5:1, 2012, 17-33.

[57] One of the recent examples of this narrative coming from the pen of a prominent thinker is found in an interview with the important Austrian social philosopher

description assumes that most or all religions have an inherent drive toward domination and ignores many crucial facts of religious history. One only has to mention that Roger Williams was moved by deep religious zeal to write freedom of religion into the constitution of his state, Rhode Island, to see the essential flaw in the common narrative.[58] And if freedom of religion is dependent on secularism, then most of humanity is doomed to never experience this fundamental freedom, for secularism never has and may never extend itself to more than a small portion of the human race. The world today is extremely religious. We need a different narrative and sociological paradigm to describe the origins of freedom of religion if this freedom is to advance.

To understand one of the ways in which freedom of religion became a supposedly secular conviction, one must notice the way in which convictions with religious roots, but which do not directly have to do with our relation with God or the divine, often migrate from the realm of religion to become themes in a broader culture to then give an orientation to economic and political behavior.[59] The phenomenon which Max Weber described in *The Protestant Ethic and the Spirit of Capitalism*, that themes of the Protestant Reformation shaped northern European thinking about work

---

Konrad Paul Liessmann, "Religionen sind ja keine Anleitung zum guten Leben," January 26, 2013, www.derStandard.at.

[58] See Thomas Schirrmacher, "Christianity and Democracy," IJRF Vol. 2:2, 2009, 73-85, for documentation.

[59] I am using a distinction between ultimate and penultimate themes in religions and worldviews, recognizing that this distinction is not always 100% clear and that the relation between the ultimate and penultimate in most religions and worldviews is dynamic. For the background for this type of analysis see Thomas K. Johnson, "Dialogue with Kierkegaard in Protestant Theology: Donald Bloesch, Francis Schaeffer, and Helmut Thielicke," MBS Text 175 (2013), available at https://www.bucer.org/resources/resources/details/mbs-texte-175-2013-dialog ue-with-kierkegaard-in-protestant-theology-donald-bloesch-francis-scha.html. In addition to responding to secular interpretations of the origins of religious freedom, the perspective I am arguing here is a response to the theory clearly articulated by Karl Marx and echoing through much of secularism, that economic relations determine our moral, cultural, and religious convictions. Already in *The Communist Manifesto* (1848) Marx claimed that class identity, which arises from economic relations, controls the convictions of a social class in such important realms as ethics, jurisprudence, family, and education. Ironically, it is the history of communism which provides some of the best evidence that economic and political behavior (including religious freedom or persecution) is heavily shaped or even controlled by the sort of convictions Marx thought were controlled by economic factors. Globally, cultural values and convictions shape and or even direct political, legal, and economic decisions.

and the economy, is not the only time this has occurred.[60] The contribution of a package of ideas and perceptions of moral duty to a culture is one of the several relations that religions have to cultures; this is one of the several relations of Christianity to culture which I advocate as a Christian theologian.[61] *This is one of the crucial roots of religious freedom in those pockets of the world's population which not only enjoy freedom of religion but also the wideranging social, moral, political, and economic benefits flowing from freedom of religion.*

There are certain ear-catching lines in the New Testament that are so poignant that they have made defining moral contributions in the history of cultures, even among people who might not accept specifically Christian claims such as the incarnation or the resurrection. For example, many perceive a direct, inherent moral authority when they hear Jesus say, "So give back to Caesar what is Caesar's, and to God what is God's" (Matthew 22:21).[62] Pontius Pilate seems to have had this experience of direct moral

---

[60] The Protestant work ethic was often summarized under the three values of "diligence, honesty, and thrift," with the background assumption that work is a calling of God, which together form a stark contrast with modern consumerism. Max Weber's study was originally published as an essay entitled "Die protestantische Ethik und der Geist des Kapitalismus" in 1904 and 1905 in volumes XX and XXI of the Archiv für Sozialwissenschaft und Sozialpolitik. It was republished in 1920 in German as the first part of Weber's series Gesammelte Aufsätze zur Religionssoziologie. It was published in English as *The Protestant Ethic and the Spirit of Capitalism*, translated by Talcott Parsons, with a foreword by R. H. Tawney (New York, Scribner, 1958; reprint New York, Dover, 2003). My application of themes from Weber to our time appeared as "The Spirit of the Protestant Work Ethic and the World Economic Crisis," MBS Text 137 (2009), https://www.bucer.de/ressource/details/mbs-texte-137-2009-the-spirit-of-the-protestant-work-ethic-and-the-world-economic-crisis.html. There have been many criticisms of Weber's thesis and of the version of it promoted by R. H. Tawney. I think the most important criticism is that Weber seriously misunderstood classical Protestant theology and especially the doctrine of election.

[61] See Thomas K. Johnson, "Christ and Culture," *Evangelical Review of Theology*, 35:1, January, 2011, https://www.academia.edu/40734562/Christ_and_Culture_2011_edition_for_the_World_Evangelical_Alliance. I have repeatedly described four dimensions of the way the biblical message relates to cultures, including correlation, critique, construction, and contribution. Cultural renewal comes by means of the combination all four relations of the biblical message to cultures.

[62] Of course, Jesus' question about "whose image" was on the coin has always led reflective hearers to consider that even Caesar was a normal mortal, created in the image of God, simultaneously undermining the cult of Caesar worship while also affirming Caesar's real but delegated authority. The biblical quotations in this paragraph undermine totalitarianism.

authority when Jesus said to him, "You would have no power over me if it were not given you from above" (John 19:11). The apostle Paul later codified these direct moral experiences into a capsule political theory when he wrote, "Let everyone be subject to the governing authorities, for there is no authority except that which God has established. The authorities that exist have been established by God" (Romans 13:1). Suddenly government authorities are perceived as having both authority from God and accountability to God, while there are also realms of human life which belong directly to God over which government has no authority; all this was communicated in such compact phrases that almost anyone can remember them, allowing many to meditate on their meaning. This is from Jesus, but Jesus did not ask these hearers to first believe something about him before accepting these foundational moral principles. These words have a direct and inherent moral authority.[63]

This is, I believe, one of the crucial cultural origins of freedom of religion. On the one hand, this moral/political package obviously has religious roots, the teaching of Jesus, but on the other hand, these moral perceptions and political convictions are not tightly tied to specific beliefs about Jesus or God, nor are they tightly tied to belonging to a particular religious community. They are the kind of convictions that are ideally suited to be transferred from the specific realm of faith into the broad stream of a moral/cultural inheritance that both leads people both to write declarations and laws protecting freedom of religion and then to perceive those declarations and laws as legitimate and worthy of enforcement. This is one of the important means of God's common grace, with a result today that some two billion people enjoy significant religious freedom, even though this work of God's grace has not yet been extended to the majority of the world's population.

If this generalized account of the historical/cultural origins of religious freedom is even partly accurate, it would be extraordinarily worthwhile to ponder how we might more consciously engage in this process that has already been going on for two millennia. Perhaps, in a generation or two, a higher percentage of our neighbors might benefit from this crucial freedom. To this end, we should glance at how these moral perceptions have been thematized historically in Christian ethics and at how we might do so in the future.

---

[63]   In this case the properly basic moral authority of these biblical statements arises from the way in which they activate moral principles which were already potentially present (but perhaps suppressed) in human consciousness because of the general revelation of God's moral law.

To avoid misunderstanding, we should say that the question we are addressing is different from the "Two Ways" doctrine that has been common in Christian ethics since the Didache; it is also different from the "Two Cities" doctrine that Augustine articulated in Christian ethics.[64] What I have in mind builds on the doctrine of Pope Gelasius I, which he articulated clearly but with a poor choice of terminology with his "Two Swords" doctrine in the 490s.

Against the Roman Empire of his time, which though in sharp decline, still had totalitarian instincts, Gelasius argued that the two authorities, church and empire, had distinct dignities with different functions which should be clarified, so that the state deals with public order, mundane matters, and temporal affairs while the church addresses divine matters and eternal mysteries. The term "Two Swords" should no longer be used; it sounds too much as if we think the church should carry a sword other than the sword of the Holy Spirit, which is the Word of God; we need to emphasize today that the state has a monopoly on the use of force which was symbolized traditionally by a physical sword. But the biblical themes which Gelasius articulated grew out of the New Testament texts we have noted and argued that civil and church authorities have their own distinct dignities and God-given responsibilities such that neither should encroach on the work of the other. The realm of faith and the realm of civic order are clearly distinguished. This is a huge conceptual step toward a theory of religious freedom coming from an early pope, which helped lay the groundwork for the development of civil society in the West.[65]

For me as a Protestant, it is fascinating to see the way themes articulated by Gelasius were developed into slightly different "Two Kingdoms" doctrines at the time of the Reformation. We can glimpse the doctrinal development from Gelasius to Luther by saying that whereas Gelasius talked about two swords, Martin Luther talked about two kingdoms, one ruled by the sword and one ruled by Christ through his Word and Spirit. For Luther, both kingdoms are really God's kingdoms, but in God's left-hand or secular

---

[64] The Didache (in Greek, Διδαχή) was a catechetical document from the late first or early second century which taught that there are two ways, a way of life and a way of death, emphasizing the difference between faith and unbelief. In his *City of God* (in Latin, *De Civitate Dei contra Paganos*), Augustine explained that humanity is comprised of two cities, one shaped by love of God and one shaped by love of self. These valuable Christian doctrines are addressing different questions from those we are addressing here.

[65] Some of this history is told effectively by David VanDrunen, *Natural Law and the Two Kingdoms: A Study in the Development of Reformed Social Thought* (Grand Rapids and Cambridge: Wm. B. Eerdmans, 2010), 21-42.

kingdom, God can remain hidden or anonymous and still accomplish his purposes for that kingdom. The left-hand kingdom is much more than government; it includes all those things that contribute to maintaining and developing earthly life, such as a marriage, family, business, stations, and property. (The inclusion of these themes other than the state distinguishes Luther's doctrine from late medieval versions of "Two Swords" theory, such as that articulated by Boniface VIII in the 1300s, which both placed business under the "Sword" of the church and claimed that the church had a type of authority over the state.) To avoid misunderstanding Luther, one must note that the kingdom rooted in creation and the kingdom rooted in redemption need each other and contribute to each other, so that the health of one is always tied to the health of the other.[66]

Perhaps more strongly than Martin Luther, John Calvin assumed a religiously unified "Christendom," a cultural situation which has long passed. Nevertheless, he contributed to two kingdoms doctrine by clarifying characteristics of each. Key attributes of the kingdom of Christ are its redemptive character, its spiritual identity, and its institutional expression in the church. Key attributes of the civil kingdom are its non-redemptive character, its earthly or external identity, and its institutional association with civil government, though it is also associated with other civic institutions. As with Luther, both kingdoms are really God's kingdoms, which must be clearly distinguished in our ethics, so that the civil kingdom is especially to be guided by God's natural moral law while the church is the place to apply *sola scriptura*.[67]

We have to face the problem that "Two Swords" and "Two Kingdoms" doctrines have repeatedly been misunderstood both among Christians and in the rest of society, even though the underlying properly basic moral apprehensions related to our New Testament quotations have been so extraordinarily constructive.[68] We commonly hear that these Christian moral doctrines mean that public life is left to secularism or to secular political ideologies, because Christian theology has become dualistic. And

---

[66] My description of Luther's views is dependent on Paul Althaus, *The Ethics of Martin Luther,* translated with a foreword by Robert C. Schultz (Philadelphia: Fortress, 1972), 43-82.
[67] See VanDrunen, 67-115.
[68] By this terminology I am suggesting we can distinguish between direct or properly basic moral and spiritual perceptions from our theoretical reflection on these perceptions. This principle of the "New Reformed Epistemology" is important for freedom of religion efforts. A good introduction to this philosophy of knowledge is Kelly James Clark, *Return to Reason: A Critique of Enlightenment Evidentialism and a Defense of Reason and Belief in God* (Grand Rapids: Wm. B. Eerdmans, 1990).

possibly some have used mistaken versions of these doctrines to claim that public officials are not directly accountable to God for their actions, the opposite of what Jesus told Pilate. However, I do not think the standard criticisms of two kingdoms doctrine are accurate. More important, I am convinced that the moral perceptions contained in two kingdoms doctrine have been crucial to the development of freedom of religion and the whole of civil society.[69]

Jesus himself distinguished between what must be given to Caesar and what must be given to God, thereby contributing a fundamental moral distinction to many cultures which has led to freedom of religion for many of us. However, we may need to update our terminology so we can communicate this distinction more effectively in Christian theology and ethics, both inside the church and also in our several cultures. For this purpose, I propose we substitute the term "Twofold Work of God in the World" in place of "Two Kingdoms Doctrine."

Under the heading of "Twofold Work of God in the World" I have suggested that we talk about six related themes in our theology and ethics. These six are: 1. God's two revelations, general revelation and special revelation; 2. The two forms in which God gives us his moral law, God's natural moral law and the biblical revelation of God's moral teaching; 3. The two types of God's grace, his common grace that makes human life possible and his special grace, meaning redemption by faith in Jesus; 4. The two types of righteousness, active civil righteousness, which is also civic responsibility, and passive spiritual righteousness, which is justification by faith in Christ; 5. Two types of wisdom, including God-given practical wisdom about how to live humane lives and spiritual wisdom of knowing God; and finally, 6. God's two kingdoms, meaning the two ways in which God reigns over our lives, including his sometimes hidden and anonymous reign over the affairs of peoples and nations through the structures of creation and his conscious redeeming reign over believers by his Word and Spirit.

An articulation of these six dualities of God's activity, rather than being dualist or secularizing, is a way to overcome many of the different dualisms that have plagued believers throughout the centuries.[70] It is very

---

[69]　The central philosophical question is if we can honestly distinguish a direct moral truth, such as Jesus' words to Pilate, from a theological truth claim, for example, that God was in Christ reconciling the world to himself. This question can also be phrased in theological terms: can we truly distinguish God's moral law from the gospel. Obviously, I think we both can and must make this distinction and should do so very clearly.

[70]　In "The Twofold Work of God in the World," MBS Text 102 (2008), I argued that a good understanding of these proper dualities overcomes many of the common

important for freedom of religion efforts: it gives us a clearly theological way of talking about life in society that is obviously *neither secular nor theocratic*. It is a theological doctrine that corresponds with what social critics such as Os Guinness are calling a "Civil Public Square," which contrasts with both a "Sacred Public Square" and a "Naked Public Square."[71] Imitating Jesus, it emphasizes that modern Pilates are directly accountable to God without saying state officials are accountable to a particular religious institution or tradition. We Christians have a way to talk about and promote freedom of religion that neither assumes secularism nor a religious establishment and which assumes that religious pluralism will continue in all the societies in which we live. We have both direct moral intuitions and an ethical theory to explain those moral intuitions, either or both of which can potentially migrate from the realm of our particular religious communities into our wider societies. This will never be complete or total, just as the northern European acceptance of the Protestant work ethic was never complete. Nevertheless, even a small and partial migration of this moral/cultural package into wider cultures would be valuable.

What to do? I think that Christian teachers from all of our traditions need to directly take up the themes of Two Kingdoms or the Twofold Work of God, both in our teaching in the Christian churches and also in all our discussions with representatives of other religions. Some other religions resist freedom of religion because they believe, unnecessarily, that freedom of religion is associated with secularism. If people who are members of other religions or members of no religion regularly hear us talk about God's twofold work and frequently hear us quote Jesus' remarkable words to Pilate or about Caesar, we may be able to slowly contribute a moral package into more and wider political cultures. In this way we might extend the wide range of social benefits related to freedom of religion to a larger number of our neighbors, even if the problem of violence and repression is a problem almost as old as humanity which will certainly continue until our Lord's return.

---

dualisms faced by Christians in the last 2000 years, including Zoroastrian, Hellenistic, nature/grace, public/private, and postmodern varieties of dualism; https://www.bucer.de/ressource/details/mbs-texte-102-2008-the-twofold-work-of-god-in-the-world.html. This argument was included in my book *What Difference Does the Trinity Make? A Complete Faith, Life, and Worldview*, vol. 7, World Evangelical Alliance Global Issues (Bonn: VKW, 2009), 33-38; https://www.iirf.eu/journal-books/global-issues-series/what-difference-does-the-trinity-make/.

[71]   See Os Guinness, *The Global Public Square Religious Freedom and the Making of a World Safe for Diversity* (IVP books, 2013).

Learning to Love the Persecuted Church[72]

What I Learned during the Global Christian Forum Consultation on Discrimination, Persecution, and Martyrdom of Christians[73]

This essay is a revised version of a sermon preached in several churches in the US and Europe shortly after I participated in the Global Christian Forum consultation on persecution. It calls us to consider the recent extreme levels of discrimination, persecution, or even martyrdom currently faced by Christians in almost every continent, described so vividly in Tirana, in the light of three passages from the New Testament: Romans 13:1–7; Revelation 13:1–10; and John 13:34–35. Because it may be helpful for the reader to review these biblical texts before reading the sermon, they are printed below. The thesis of the sermon is that Christians in the mostly free regions of the world have much to learn about how to love Christians in regions typified by greater persecution, and that beginning this process of learning is a test of our discipleship as followers of Jesus.

Romans 13:1–7

> Let everyone be subject to the governing authorities, for there is no authority except that which God has established. The authorities that exist have been established by God. Consequently, whoever rebels against the authority is rebelling against what God has instituted, and those who do so will bring judgment on themselves. For rulers hold no terror for those who do right, but for those who do wrong. Do you want to be free from fear of the

---

[72] This essay was originally a sermon preached at several churches in Europe and the US. It was first published as "Learning to Love the Persecuted Church: With the Message of the Tirana Consultation on Discrimination, Persecution, and Martyrdom," MBS Text 186 (2016), https://www.bucer.de/ressource/details/mbs-texte-186-2016-learning-to-love-the-persecuted-church.html. It was also published in *Sharing of Faith Stories*, edited by Richard Howell on behalf of the Global Christian Forum (New Delhi, India: Caleb Institute of Theology, 2018), 421-434.

[73] This consultation was held in Tirana, Albania, 1 to 5 November 2015. A comprehensive report on the event was published as *Discrimination, Persecution, Martyrdom: Following Christ Together*, edited by Huibert van Beek and Larry Miller, with an introduction by Larry Miller (Bonn: VKW, 2018), https://globalchristianforum.org/wp-content/uploads/2020/10/Tirana_Report_DPM_Consultation-1.pdf.

one in authority? Then do what is right and you will be commended. For the one in authority is God's servant for your good. But if you do wrong, be afraid, for rulers do not bear the sword for no reason. They are God's servants, agents of wrath to bring punishment on the wrongdoer. Therefore, it is necessary to submit to the authorities, not only because of possible punishment but also as a matter of conscience. This is also why you pay taxes, for the authorities are God's servants, who give their full time to governing. Give to everyone what you owe them: If you owe taxes, pay taxes; if revenue, then revenue; if respect, then respect; if honor, then honor.

Revelation 13:1–10

The dragon stood on the shore of the sea. And I saw a beast coming out of the sea. It had ten horns and seven heads, with ten crowns on its horns, and on each head a blasphemous name. The beast I saw resembled a leopard, but had feet like those of a bear and a mouth like that of a lion. The dragon gave the beast his power and his throne and great authority. One of the heads of the beast seemed to have had a fatal wound, but the fatal wound had been healed. The whole world was filled with wonder and followed the beast. People worshiped the dragon because he had given authority to the beast, and they also worshiped the beast and asked, "Who is like the beast? Who can wage war against it?" The beast was given a mouth to utter proud words and blasphemies and to exercise its authority for forty-two months. It opened its mouth to blaspheme God, and to slander his name and his dwelling place and those who live in heaven. It was given power to wage war against God's holy people and to conquer them. And it was given authority over every tribe, people, language and nation. All inhabitants of the earth will worship the beast—all whose names have not been written in the Lamb's book of life, the Lamb who was slain from the creation of the world. Whoever has ears, let them hear. "If anyone is to go into captivity, into captivity they will go. If anyone is to be killed with the sword, with the sword they will be killed." This calls for patient endurance and faithfulness on the part of God's people.

John 13:34–35

Jesus said, "A new command I give you: Love one another. As I have loved you, so you must love one another. By this everyone will know that you are my disciples, if you love one another."

In 2007 a young Turkish man, the father of two children, was planning to take a theology class that I was scheduled to teach when he was brutally martyred. Two other Christians, one Turkish and one German, were also murdered with him in the office of their Bible printing shop in

Turkey. They were cut up with knives! I felt like I had been kicked in the stomach when I first read what had happened. Shocked and angry, I became deeply involved in reporting on and drawing attention to this terrible incident.

Afterward I felt compelled (by God, I think) to consider how Christians face discrimination, persecution, and sometimes even martyrdom in many countries around the world. This included thinking about the different types of governments we see in different countries, since governments usually have some important role in relation to discrimination and persecution. I also contemplated our international duties within the Body of Christ, since we now live in a post-globalization world. This message shares some of what I have learned.

We find in the New Testament two complementary views of the state or of government, which we must hold together in our minds and in the practice of Christian discipleship. On one hand, Romans 13 describes what a state **should** be and do. This passage is very comfortable for us who live in free countries, where we have official protection of human rights and the rule of law. "The one in authority is God's servant for your good. But if you do wrong, be afraid, for rulers do not bear the sword for no reason." Therefore, we should generally obey the law and pay our taxes.

But on the other hand, in Revelation 13, we have a description of what a state or a government can become when everything goes wrong. A state can become a devouring beast, destroying everything in its path, and especially attacking Christians with demonic hatred. This was not only the experience of the church in the first century, under the persecutions by Nero in the sixties and Domitian in the eighties; it is also the experience of tens of millions of Christians today. A few months ago I attended a meeting with representatives of persecuted churches from dozens of countries.[74] When someone claimed that the slaughter of Christians in Syria and Iraq should be called genocide, no one disagreed. On the contrary, Christians from other countries responded by saying that what was happening in their nations should be considered genocide too! We may have multiple Christian genocides occurring right now at the hands of multiple beastly governments. The beast of Revelation 13 is not just a reality from ancient history; **the beast is back!**

In this light, we Christians who live in free countries, where the government generally fulfills Paul's vision in Romans 13, need to carefully consider the challenging words of Jesus in John 13:34–35: "A new command I give you: Love one another. As I have loved you, so you must love one

---

[74]   This was the Tirana consultation in November 2015.

another. By this everyone will know that you are my disciples, if you love one another."

A generation ago, Francis Schaeffer taught us that visible love is the mark of a Christian, basing his teaching on Jesus' words in John 13.[75] Jesus has given our unbelieving neighbors, called "everyone" here, the astonishing right to evaluate our claim to be disciples of Jesus. They are to make this evaluation on the basis of our love for fellow Christians. Therefore, this love must be more than a feeling; it must become visible as sacrificial action for fellow Christians in need. In our largely globalized society, we need to fully engage with what it means for Christians in the free world to honestly love fellow Christians who live under a variety of beasts. We have much to learn.

As we learn how to love Christians living under the beast, we should also consider what this will do for us. I suppose that many of us in the free world are a bit lukewarm about the gospel. We take the gospel and the church for granted, as if they are not so special. One of the benefits of honestly engaging with persecuted Christians is that it may break us out of our spiritual lethargy. How can one remain unmoved when hearing or reading stories of martyrdom and of tens of thousands of our brothers and sisters in Christ fleeing for their lives? Initiatives that change the situation for persecuted believers may also have a large effect on us!

An additional benefit is that such engagement with persecuted Christians may prepare us for problems in our own countries. In the free world, we do not have hundreds of martyrs or thousands fleeing for their lives, but we do sometimes face real and serious discrimination on account of our faith.[76] And we do not know what the future will be for those of us who now enjoy freedom. Many Christians now facing severe persecution did not expect it in their countries just a few decades ago. In some parts of the world we observe a progression: discrimination leads to persecution, which leads to martyrdom. Getting involved with Christians facing persecution may equip us to face discrimination, which could escalate at some point to become persecution for us too. And never forget: this love in action will be noticed by a watching world, leading some to consider Jesus, whose disciples we have proved to be.

---

[75] See Francis Schaeffer, *The Mark of the Christian* (L'Abri Fellowship, 1970), now available from InterVarsity Press.

[76] An example would be the way the radical gay rights movement has challenged the legal status of some Christian institutions because they teach traditional values. Discrimination against Christians in the free world is usually because of the application of Christian ethics to public questions, not because of attending a worship service.

A word about Romans 13: Paul is presenting a very compressed version of a political theory that merits extensive explanation. For now, I will simply note that Paul assumed several other themes and texts in the Bible. For example, he assumed what Jesus said in Matthew 22:21: "So give to Caesar what is Caesar's, and to God what is God's." Paul also assumed what Jesus said to Pilate in John 19:11: "You would have no power over me if it were not given to you from above." And Paul clearly thought that most people serving in government can distinguish between good and evil, so that usually states can attempt to punish the evil and reward the good, even if very imperfectly. And there are other biblical assumptions underlying what both Jesus and Paul said about government: the creation of humans in God's image, the fallenness of each person, the existence of an objective moral law, and the authority of written documents.

When we look around the world today and see where Christians and others enjoy a significant level of freedom of religion and other basic human rights protections, I think I see a pattern. I see the influence of the biblical themes assumed in Romans 13 upstream in the culture and educational systems, as a condition of the current experience of freedom and human rights protections. It is not by accident that some countries enjoy freedom and other countries do not. In countries where the people enjoy freedom, even if the populace does not widely acknowledge Jesus as their Savior, there has usually been some significant influence of a few key ideas from the Bible within the last few hundred years. It is the cultural influence of the Bible being felt in the political sphere. I have begun to think of this part of the world as "the Romans 13 world." People in this world believe there is a realm of life that does not belong to Caesar. They may believe that modern Pilates are accountable to God for their actions. They may believe that people have a special dignity, even if they do not know the source this dignity. They believe that even top government officials should obey written laws. Most of us reading this message live in this world.[77]

Now a word about Revelation 13. There have been so many wildly speculative theories about the beast or the dragon or the antichrist that

---

[77] Recently I read a fascinating account of an official from Communist China who had heard that Christians prayed the communists out of power in East Germany in 1980. This official was afraid that Christians would also pray the Chinese communists out of power! I see this as an example of the influence of a biblical theme, the direct accountability of all people to God, even among people who do not yet acknowledge that they believe in God — in this case, a Chinese communist official who probably had to profess atheism. This account is found in a report written by Thomas Schirrmacher for the WEA Religious Liberty Commission.

responsible theologians may hesitate to mention these themes at all. That would be a mistake. It is beyond the scope of this message to offer a complete interpretation of the book of Revelation, but I think that the apostle John was giving us a pictorial interpretation of events of his time, designed to help believers throughout history to respond to similar events.

In the decades before John wrote this text, as already noted, Christians endured two waves of persecution, under the emperors Nero and Domitian.[78] Though there were probably differences between the two, in both cases the Roman Empire became beast-like. The first period of persecution, under Nero, probably lasted about 42 months, until his death and a change of government. Tradition claims that both Peter and Paul were martyred under Nero, making it an especially painful time for Christians. I think the apostle John lost trusted friends during Nero's persecution. John saw both of these persecutions as ultimately instigated by Satan, represented by the dragon. In John's lifetime, Satan had repeatedly attempted to use a beast-like government to destroy Christians and the churches. The beasts he described were not speculation about some mysterious time in the future; they were his depiction of what the churches had experienced but presented in such a manner as to prepare future Christians for what would happen again.

John also mentions a false prophet in another chapter; I think this refers to the redevelopment of emperor worship at his time in history. Some people within the Roman Empire were afraid that the empire would completely fall apart, leading to chaos and poverty. They thought that the religion of emperor worship, along with a very powerful emperor, would unify and save their society. The religion of emperor worship served as an ideological justification for an all-powerful emperor. The Roman Empire would take control of everything external in society while the religion of emperor worship would get inside people's hearts and minds, leaving no place that belongs only to God and not to Caesar. In this way, the false prophet, representing false religion, gave spiritual support to a beastly government.

What we must notice here is that the central creed of the early Christians, that "Jesus is Lord," was the exact opposite and denial of the central creed of emperor worship, "Caesar is Lord." Both were claims to be lord of

---

[78] There has long been a historians' debate whether John wrote the book of Revelation about AD 95 or about AD 68, before the destruction of Jerusalem. Following what I take to be the view of Irenaeus (AD 132–202), I think that the later date is more likely, but this difference has little effect on the theme of this message, except that John would not yet have experienced Domitian's persecution.

everything in life; both were foundations of a complete worldview and approach to life. When the combination of the Roman Empire and emperor worship became totalitarian, claiming the people's whole heart, mind, and life, it came into complete spiritual and moral conflict with Christians and the biblical message.

Recently I heard a very moving speech by a Christian woman from Syria, describing what she had seen and experienced in the last few years. I obtained a printed copy of her speech so that I can quote her accurately. It shows us that the beast described by the apostle John in Revelation 13 is not only ancient history. A state, or supposed state, acting like a devouring beast is the experience of many Christians today. Pay attention to the words of Mrs. Rosangela Jarjour, Secretary General of the Fellowship of Middle East Evangelical Churches:

- "From the Christian quarters of al Hamidiya and Bustan el Diwan in the old city of Homs, the city where I spent my childhood and teenage, more than 80,000 Christians were cleansed from their homes in early 2012, and their homes were occupied by the militant rebels (al Farouq brigade).
- Eight kilometers away from my parents' village lies Saddad, a peaceful town that was mentioned twice in the Bible. The townspeople lived peacefully for tens of years until late October 2013, when both the Free Syrian Army and Al Nusra Front attacked Saddad and brutally murdered 53 civilians, including an entire family of six who were blindfolded, shot in the head, and thrown in a well.
- The 100th Anniversary of the Armenian Genocide was commemorated in Aleppo with the Islamic factions' leveling to the ground of seven buildings in Al-Suleimania Christian neighborhood on Good Friday (April 10, 2015). Twenty-nine Christians lost their lives and 56 were injured. Easter Sunday was the day to mourn the dead family members and relatives as the whole town was in deep shock.
- Only three weeks before that, 179 Christian families lost shelter and all possessions after al Nusra Front stormed the city of Idlib. Of these families, only 85% of the Christians were able to flee, with their women wearing Islamic robes and hijabs; the others faced an unknown fate.
- The daily mortar and missile attacks by the so-called Moderate rebels on Meharda and the Christian neighborhoods of Damascus and Aleppo have claimed hundreds of innocent Christian civilians' lives — among them children in attacks on schools and nurseries.
- The Christian population of 400,000 in Aleppo, many of Armenian descent, had already been reduced to an estimated 45,000 by March 2015.

- In the North, 30 Christian Assyrian villages were attacked and wiped out. Many were massacred, and the rest either became IDPs or left the country. Up till this minute, 200 families are still held hostages by ISIS.
- For many Christians in Syria, it has become commonplace for Islamic extremists, including ISIS and Syrian rebels, to storm Christian neighborhoods, towns, and villages; destroy their churches, tear down their crosses, and deface their icons and murals; and kidnap Christians for ransom or murder them. Those Christians, who chose to live peacefully on their ancestors' land, are now being eradicated by merciless militants for no other reason than being followers of the Christian faith while the Western world has remained silent and even reluctant to listen to their voices or answer to their intense suffering."[79]

When I thought about her words, I wished I could tell her that the persecution of her group of Christians will only last another few months, to reach the 42 months referred to in the book of Revelation. But I do not think that this reference is a literal promise that all severe persecutions will end in that period of time. Maybe the 42 months mentioned by the apostle John were meant to describe the time of intense persecution under Emperor Nero in the first century; maybe they are symbolic of a limited period of time, not to be taken too literally. Therefore, on the basis of the Bible, I do not think we can tell Mrs. Jarjour that the Syrians' time of tribulation is almost over. I am not sure that would be true.

What I am sure of is that today millions of Christians are living under the beast, in a Revelation 13 world, while we live in a Romans 13 world, enjoying freedoms that are partly the result of the Bible's influence on our world. And Jesus has told us that the watching world will know that we are disciples of Jesus by the way in which we love each other, including the group of Christians to which Mrs. Jarjour belongs.

I am sure we are all wondering what we can do that will truly help Christians in Syria and Iraq. But before we consider that question, I should mention that the Christians in Syria and Iraq are not the Christians under the highest level of persecution today. The story gets worse.

About three years ago, in 2013, I participated in an international consultation on religious freedom research in Istanbul, Turkey. Many had perceived that the persecution of Christians in many countries was getting

---

[79] English grammar and sentence structure have been lightly corrected with no change of content. This speech was given at the consultation held in Tirana, November 2015. Her entire speech is found in *Discrimination, Persecution, Martyrdom*, 82-85, https://globalchristianforum.org/wp-content/uploads/2020/10/Tirana_Report_DPM_Consultation-1.pdf.

worse, so 40 or 50 researchers and activists gathered to discuss the problems. We quickly realized that Christians from around the world and across traditions within Christendom needed to cooperate much more extensively in responding to growing persecution. Consequently, the World Evangelical Alliance, working with the Vatican, the World Council of Churches, and the Pentecostal World Fellowship, called a meeting of representatives of persecuted churches. Because we were concerned about an ISIS attack, we held this meeting secretly in Albania in November 2015. About 70 representatives of persecuted churches and about 75 representatives of churches in the free world attended.

My role in this event was that of senior editor; this means that, with a team, I edited the books that we specially printed to give to the delegates who attended. As part of this effort, we combined information and analysis from evangelical and Roman Catholic researchers about the status and causes of persecution in the 50 worst countries around the world. While I was working on these data, studying stories of terrible brutality, I sometimes felt sick to my stomach. One day I looked to see where my waste basket was, in case I began vomiting at my desk. But we confirmed important patterns among the causes of Christian persecution. For example, at that time, in 78% of the 50 worst countries where Christians were under serious persecution, one of the main causes, often combined with another cause, was some type of extremist Islam (though there are very different types of Islamic extremism). In several other countries, the leading cause of the persecution of Christians is some type of Hindu or Buddhist nationalism. And in a few places, the main cause of the persecution of Christians is organized crime or simple corruption. But the country with the worst level of persecution of Christians is North Korea.

In the past few years I have met representatives of persecuted Christians from some surprising places — surprising in the sense that I did not expect those people to be able to travel so freely: Syria, Iraq, Iran, Nepal, Kurdistan, Kazakhstan, Vietnam, Cambodia, or China. But I have never met a Christian from North Korea. Not many Christians from North Korea are able to travel to tell their story, but the reports I have heard suggest that the combination of communism with a personality cult makes a ferocious beast.

But what should we do? What is the duty of love that Christians in the Romans 13 world owe to Christians in the Revelation 13 world? One of the purposes of the meeting in Albania was for leaders and researchers from churches in the free world to listen to leaders from the persecuted church, so that we could develop better "to do" lists. Love must be practical. Two types of "to do" lists were developed in the meetings, one oriented toward churches and the other toward the world. I think these lists are extremely valuable and must be implemented in our circles. But two matters seemed so important that they came before practical "to do" lists.

Our first duty is prayer for the persecuted churches. Even if we do not know much about their theology, ethics, and worship, we can pray for them. As I have listened in person to the prayer requests from persecuted Christians, two themes have caught my ear. The first is the fear that they will be forgotten or abandoned by other Christians. They do not want to die for their faith without other Christians knowing about their martyrdom. The second theme is their prayer request for boldness in witness and proclamation while many of their members are being killed. I have heard people say, "Pray that we would be bold till we die, so that there will still be a church in our country to bring the gospel to our neighbors after this time of persecution is past." I think it is appropriate to include prayer for persecuted Christians in private, in our families, and in our normal congregational prayer, as well as to have special Lord's Days dedicated to prayer for the persecuted churches.

The second matter that seemed to come before a practical "to do" list was to address our tragic Christian history of internal intra-Christian persecution. At the suggestion of the Pope, our Roman Catholic colleagues took the lead in asking us to say: "We repent of having at times persecuted each other and other religious communities in history, and we ask forgiveness from each other and pray for new ways of following Christ together."

In this context, it seemed clear that the Roman Catholic Church had openly repented to Evangelicals and Protestants for their role in persecuting them in the past. This repentance was accepted by Evangelicals and Protestants at the meeting. I see this as a result of the work of the Holy Spirit. The era of intra-Christian persecution should be past. This achievement was of extreme value, and by itself this made the time and treasure invested in the meetings worthwhile. The history of Christians persecuting other Christians has been forgiven. In principle, internal Christian persecution should be finished!

Some other themes in our Tirana "to do" lists are important and must be implemented. We said:

"In communion with Christ we commit ourselves:
(a) To listen more to the experiences of Christians, Churches, and of all those who are discriminated against and persecuted, and deepen our engagement with suffering communities.

(b) To pray more for Churches, for Christians, and for all those suffering discrimination and persecution, as well as for the transformation of those who discriminate and persecute.

(c) To speak up more with respect and dignity, with a clear and strong voice together, on behalf of those who are suffering.

(d) To do more in mutual understanding to find effective ways of solidarity and support for healing, for reconciliation, and for the religious freedom of all oppressed and persecuted people."

The second "to do" list coming from the Albania consultation was oriented toward the world, and it includes the types of things that should, in my opinion, work gradually — over the very long term — to help in changing Revelation 13 countries into Romans 13 countries. To quote from this list, the consultation called on:

"*All persecutors* who discriminate against and oppress Christians and violate human rights to cease their abuse and to affirm the right of all human beings to life and dignity.

All governments to respect and protect the freedom of religion and belief of all people as a fundamental human right. We also appeal to governments and international organizations to respect and protect Christians and all other people of goodwill from threats and violence committed in the name of religion. In addition, we ask them to work for peace and reconciliation, to seek the settlement of ongoing conflicts, and to stop the flow of arms, especially to violators of human rights.

All media to report in an appropriate and unbiased way on violations of religious freedom, including the discrimination and persecution of Christians as well as of other faith communities.

All educational institutions to develop opportunities and tools to teach young people in particular about human rights, religious tolerance, healing of memories and hostilities of the past, and peaceful means of conflict resolution and reconciliation."

We have to see the significance of these words. Representatives of almost all the organizations in the world that call themselves Christian churches were calling on the other main institutions in society, government, media, and education to take up their proper roles to reduce the persecution of Christians and related human rights abuses. This is not something we can do in five minutes after church. This requires serious long-term efforts by people responsible for our churches, government, media, and educational institutions. And, I believe, these duties fall especially on those Christians and churches that have a rich intellectual and educational history, and that therefore can figure out how to express effective love for persecuted Christians in government, the media, and education.

Keep in mind what I claimed a few minutes ago: the governments in the Romans 13 world usually have some important moral influences upstream of what they decide to do today. In many or most of the countries with religious freedom, somewhere in the last 200 years, there was a significant influence of some biblical themes — perhaps about human dignity, perhaps about freedom of conscience before God. We have to use the means of church, government, media, and education to try to make that happen for Christians in the Revelation 13 world. Many researchers think the persecution of Christians around the world has become much worse in the last five years. Multiple beasts have returned. We should use all legitimate means to respond.

What should you do, personally or with your church? Let me give some suggestions:

1. Pray!
2. Start to read about the problem. My favorite source for reliable information is the World Watch List, which provides both shorter and longer reports about the countries where religious persecution is extreme.[80] For many years I have helped to develop the books, journals, and various reports published by the International Institute for Religious Freedom; we have a growing body of serious literature written by our researchers that addresses many dimensions of the problem.[81]
3. Start to learn about human rights documents and principles. At least since the United Nations endorsed the Universal Declaration of Human Rights (1948), freedom of religion has been regarded as an important human right, even if many nations ignore it. It would be a worthwhile step if all Christians knew something about human rights.
4. Ask what your government says and does in regard to religious freedom and persecution. Do not be surprised if your government is not completely consistent with its own principles. Ask your officials if they are implementing their own principles in both domestic and foreign policy.

---

[80] https://www.opendoorsusa.org/christian-persecution/world-watch-list/.
[81] http://iirf.eu/.

5. Ask if your school or university should do something more educationally with regard to human rights and religious freedom.
6. Ask if your church could develop a partnership with a particular persecuted church.

I hope that the location of our November consultation on discrimination, persecution, and martyrdom might be an encouragement to persecuted Christians. We held it in Albania, not only for security reasons but also to celebrate the fact that the terrible persecution under communism has ended. Albania itself would have been near the top of the list of persecuting countries a generation ago. For many years during that country's totalitarian regime, it was effectively illegal not to be an atheist.[82] But this changed with the end of communism, so that there is now a good level of freedom of religion in Albania. Severe persecution often comes to an end; freedom often returns. With this in mind, I would like you to conclude reading this essay by praying for the persecuted church, keeping in mind the requests I have heard from persecuted Christians.

---

[82] This policy direction began during the closing months of World War II and reached its high point in Albanian law in the constitution of 1976 and the penal code of 1977. The ban on religion was effectively reduced in 1985, and since 1990 Albania has enjoyed a good level of religious freedom. The efforts of Mother Teresa contributed to the transition.

Appendix by Pavel Hošek:

The Human Rights Theories of Božena Komárková and Thomas K. Johnson:[83]

Two Views of the Relation between Universal Human Rights and the Natural Moral Law within Christian Thought

In this article the author analyzes and compares two contrary perspectives on the role of natural moral law in Christian ethics, especially in Christian public claims for universally valid moral principles and values such as those underlying the concept of universal human rights and the corresponding notion of religious freedom. The first perspective under consideration is presented in the published works of the Czech Christian human rights activist and defender of religious freedom Božena Komárková; the second perspective is presented in the writings of the American Reformed theologian Thomas K. Johnson.

Key words: human rights, natural law, Christian ethics

Freedom of religion is generally considered to be one of the basic "universal human rights." Since the human rights discourse has become widely accepted and influential in the contemporary world, Christians engaged in defending their own or other peoples' freedom of religion have to think through the relation between Christianity and universal human rights, and, in particular, they have to decide whether they should use the worldwide consensus concerning human rights and support their claim for religious freedom in public debates by referring to generally acknowledged and accepted sets of universal human rights, including the right for freedom of religion. In this article, I want to present and

---

[83] Pavel Hošek, Th.D., is a professor at the Faculty of Evangelical Theology at Charles University whose research focuses on the relationship between theology and culture, religion, and interfaith dialogue. This essay was originally published in the *International Journal for Religious Freedom*, Vol. 5:2, 2012 as "The Christian claim for universal human rights in relation to the natural moral law: A comparison and contrast of the thought of Božena Komárková and Thomas K. Johnson."

compare two alternative ways of substantiating the Christian claim for universal human rights and freedom of religion in relation to the notion of natural moral law.

Christianity and human rights

The relation between Christian theology and the idea of universal human rights is very complex, both historically and conceptually.[84] In the contemporary world, many Christian organizations support and defend the rights of people who suffer from human rights violations, such as denying or limiting freedom of religion, whether the people in view are fellow Christians or adherents of other faiths. On the other hand, many Christian churches and individual theologians have opposed the concept of universal human rights, including freedom of religion, as theologically wrong and unacceptable. Moreover, in countries with a strong coalition between the majority church and the political establishment, the rights of some groups and individuals (especially freedom of religion) have been denied, and in some countries this continues today. Some human rights activists actually see religion (Christian or any other) primarily as a problem – as a source of justification for those who legitimize their abuse of power and their violations of human rights. Some of these activists also suggest that the greatest enemy of religious freedom is, in fact – religion. Yet, at the same time, many other human rights activists suggest that if we give up on a religious, theological foundation and justification of human rights, including freedom of religion, we are weakening our claim for their universal validity and applicability.[85]

This is why many Christian theologians emphasize theological and spiritual values that have played an essential role in identifying, defining, and shaping human rights in European and American history. But there is one very important disagreement among Christian thinkers, who emphasize the specifically Judeo-Christian origin of the concept of universal human rights, including freedom of religion. Some of them refer just to the Bible (and its understanding of God and humanity) to substantiate their

[84] For a general summary of issues involved, see William Brackney, *Human Rights and the World's Major Religions: The Christian Tradition* (London: Praeger Perspectives, 2005).

[85] See, for example, Max Stackhouse, "Human Rights and Public Theology," in *Religion and Human Rights. Competing Claims?* edited by Carrie Gustafson and Peter Juviler (New York: M. E. Sharpe, 1999), and Max Stackhouse, "Sources and Prospects for Human Rights Ideas: A Christian Perspective," in *The Idea of Human Rights: Traditions and Presence*, edited by Jindřich Halama (Praha: ETF UK, 2003), 194, 199.

claim for universal validity of human rights and refuse to support their argument by any reference to a universally recognizable natural law of morality. Others believe that to make a Christian claim for universal human rights (and the corresponding claim for religious freedom) plausible, even for those who do not share Christian faith, a reference to some kind of universally human basis of morality, such as the Stoic notion of "natural law," is legitimate and, in fact, necessary. In this article I am going to present and compare these two conflicting views, the first represented by a Czech Christian human rights activist and defender of religious freedom, Božena Komárková (1903-1997), the second represented by an American Reformed theologian, Thomas K. Johnson.

Božena Komárková: the Christian origin of human rights

In many of her writings Božena Komárková emphasized what she considers as unquestionable evidence for the biblical and theological roots of human rights and the notion of religious freedom.[86] She always claimed that the whole concept of human rights and religious freedom was inspired by Judeo-Christian biblical and theological values and teachings, and, in particular, by the Calvinist stream of the Reformation in its Anglo-Saxon form.[87] She also claimed that this was not a matter of historical coincidence, in other words, that this theological origin of human rights and the concept of religious freedom has to be acknowledged and emphasized, because if it is forgotten, denied, or viewed as coincidental and unnecessary, the whole concept of universal human rights with their unconditional validity will lose its essential foundation and may not survive.[88] Human rights without substantiation in theology, i.e., without reference to the transcendent guarantee of human dignity, is an extremely vulnerable concept.[89] Human rights and religious freedom must be viewed in the context of God's covenantal relationship with humanity. They must be understood in relation to God's call to freedom, responsibility, and obedience.[90] Only if

---

[86]   See especially her book *Lidská práva* (Heršpice: Eman, 1997), her *Původ a význam lidských práv* (Praha: SPN, 1990), and an English translation of her papers related to human rights, Komárková, *Human Rights and the Rise of the Secular Age* (Heršpice: Eman, 1991), referenced below as HRRSA.

[87]   Cf. Pavel Keřkovský, Introduction, *Human Rights and the Rise of the Secular Age*, 15; see also Komárková, "Human Rights and Christianity," HRRSA, 69, 72, and 82.

[88]   Komárková, "Are Christian Institutions Possible?" HRRSA, 42; see also "Three Observations," HRRSA, 180.

[89]   Komárková, "The Reformation and the Modern State," HRRSA, 129.

[90]   Komárková, "Human Rights and Christianity," HRRSA, 70.

we anchor human rights in God's will for humankind can we insist on their universal and unconditional validity.[91] Human rights are not created or issued by the state. They only make sense with reference to God who revealed Himself to humanity in Christ.[92]

Even though the logic of Komárková's argument seems sound and convincing, she and those Christians who make this claim have to face a serious difficulty. In the contemporary context of cultural and religious pluralism, insisting on a very close tie between human rights and a particular type of Christian theology may make it quite difficult to convince others about their universal applicability – especially those outside the Christian community.[93] In many of her articles, Komárková argues again and again that there is sufficient historical evidence that human rights as they appeared in Europe and America have been derived from particular spiritual values of the Judeo-Christian tradition, more precisely, from its Anglo-Saxon Calvinist Protestant form. She claims again and again that without these religious values, human rights cannot stand in the long-term perspective. She insists that if human rights and the corresponding notion of religious freedom are viewed simply as a legal matter, as a consensus of a particular society, without reference to any guarantee transcending all human institutions and societies, they can be changed and abolished by political authorities just as they were accepted. But how does such an understanding of human rights relate to Hindus, Buddhists, or Muslims? Can one say something significant about human rights in societies without such Judeo-Christian historical roots?

There is no question that Komárková's argument has actually been quite effective and fully intelligible in her central European context because of its strong Judeo-Christian cultural heritage. In fact, she was a courageous human rights activist and defender of religious freedom in Communist Czechoslovakia, challenging the totalitarian government of this country for human rights violations and severe limitations of religious freedom, and she was persecuted by the Communist government on that account.[94] Her arguments were meaningful for her central European listeners and readers, both Christian and secular. After all, she was speaking to an audience that shared the history to which she was referring; the history leading up to formulating the human rights declarations and charters

---

[91]   Komárková, "Human Rights and Christianity," 99.
[92]   Komárková, "Are Christian Institutions Possible?" HRRSA, 42.
[93]   Cf. Stackhouse, "Sources and Prospects for Human Rights Ideas: A Christian Perspective," p. 183ff.
[94]   See Keřkovský, Introduction, *Human Rights and the Rise of the Secular Age*, 7ff.

defending religious freedom was in a significant sense their history, which was true even of those who did not share her Christian faith. All her readers knew what she meant by the word "human" in the phrase "human rights," and all her readers basically agreed with that concept of humanity. But what if she spoke to Buddhists or Hindus? What if she spoke to Muslims? How would her insistence on the Christian theological origin of human rights change her claim for their universal validity in a religiously plural context, i.e., in today's social and political reality in both Europe and America, not to mention other parts of the world?

Komárková is obviously right in claiming that the universal validity and unconditional applicability of human rights is better substantiated if it is anchored in theology, i.e., in God's universal will for humankind, than if it should just be based on human governments and their unpredictable decisions.[95] Yet, at the same time, the way Komárková links human rights and their origin with a specific theological tradition (Anglo-Saxon Calvinist Protestantism) makes it very difficult to persuade non-Europeans and non-Christians of their universal applicability. The fact that human rights are derived from one particular tradition might seemingly limit their relevance for those who do not share the accepted religious values of that tradition or who were not raised in a cultural environment shaped by these values. Religious pluralism in the contemporary world is a serious challenge for any universal claim, especially if that universalist claim is derived from such particular theological presuppositions.

Historically speaking, there is no question that many important Judeo-Christian values have played a very significant role in the discussions leading to the formulation of the most important human rights declarations, such as the US Declaration of Independence in 1776, the French Declaration of the rights of man and of the citizen in 1789 (very much influenced, in fact, by the American Declaration of Independence), and also the United Nations Universal Declaration of Human Rights in 1948.[96]

However, the more evidence we bring for the decisive Jewish-Christian influence on the rise and development of human rights discourse in Western culture, the more we are faced with the problem of their universal validity and applicability. If human rights are intrinsically tied with a "Western," "Euro-American," or "Judeo-Christian" history and particularity, why

---

[95] Cf. also Thomas K. Johnson, "Human Rights and Christian Ethics," in *Communio Viatorum*, III./2005, 329; see also his *Human Rights: A Christian Primer* (Bonn: VKW, 2008), 61f.

[96] Cf. Stackhouse, "Sources and Prospects for Human Rights Ideas: A Christian Perspective," 186f; see also Johnson, "Human Rights and Christian Ethics," 326.

should we expect them to be viewed as valid and binding for Buddhists or Hindus or Muslims? Why should Japanese or Chinese or Pakistani people feel obliged by a document based on Euro-American Christian theology?

Religious pluralism and different understandings of humanity

In trying to answer this question, we have to acknowledge the fact that in speaking about "human" rights as a universal concept, we are actually using the adjective "human" in a normative sense, which implies a particular sort of anthropology (i.e., a particular view of what the word "human" means). And here we face a problem, which does not seem to be sufficiently addressed in Komárková's proposal. The problem is that each cultural and religious tradition has its own particular view of humanity, i.e., its own normative anthropology, based in its sacred texts. Let us look shortly at the Muslim, Hindu, and Buddhist understandings of humanity to see some of the most obvious similarities and differences in comparison with the Judeo-Christian anthropology, which has had, as we have seen, a strong impact on the rise and development of universal human rights discourse in Western culture.

In the Islamic tradition, the general understanding of human nature is similar to that in Jewish and Christian anthropology. In spite of that similarity, the Islamic view of humanity is unique. In Islamic sacred texts and their later normative interpretations, we find a very specific understanding of human beings: every man and woman is born as a "Muslim," i.e., with an innate inclination to be submitted to and obedient to the Creator. Each and every human being should therefore live in accordance with the revealed law of human behavior (*shariah*). Human dignity, sanctity of human life and equality of all human beings, gender roles, and family structures, for example, are all based on these theological presuppositions.[97] In Islamic sacred texts (Qur'an and *sunna*), we find many principles and ideas similar to those underlying the 1948 UN Declaration of human rights.[98] At

---

[97]   Cf. Roger Garaudy, "Human Rights in Islam: Foundation, Tradition, Violation," in *The Ethics of World Religions and Human Rights*, edited by Hans Küng and Jürgen Moltmann (London: SCM Press, 1990), 46ff. See also Thomas K. Johnson, "The Twofold Work of God in the World," MBS Text 102 (2008), 5, available here: https://www.bucer.de/ressource/details/mbs-texte-102-2008-the-twofold-work-of-god-in-the-world.html.

[98]   Cf. Riffat Hassan, "On Human Rights and the Quranic Perspective," *Human Rights in Religious Traditions*, edited by Arlene Swidler (New York: The Pilgrim Press, 1982), 51ff. See also RA Jullundhri, "Human Rights and Islam," in *Understanding*

the same time, Islamic interpretations of Qur'an and *sunna* are in certain areas in quite obvious tension with how human rights are understood in Western countries,[99] especially in areas such as, for example, the social role of women,[100] the status and treatment of non-Muslims, religious freedom. The fact that Muslims have serious objections to the UN Declaration of human rights has actually led some of their leaders to formulating and publishing specifically Islamic declarations of human rights in accordance with Muslim faith and tradition.[101]

The Islamic view of humanity, as we have seen, is therefore not exactly the same as the implicit anthropology of the 1948 UN Declaration.[102] And, whereas Judaism, Christianity, and Islam have (in spite of significant differences) many things in common, since all three are monotheistic religions and all three refer to Abraham and the ancient Israelite patriarchs as their forefathers, in the case of the two most well-known religious traditions which have their roots in India, Hinduism and Buddhism, we encounter a completely different framework.

In the Hindu tradition, which is in itself very diverse and multifarious, man is a (potentially) divine being, temporarily imprisoned in this material world, a being whose individual destiny is determined by *karma*. The quality of one's *karma* depends on how that person has lived in previous lives. The goal of human existence is to achieve ultimate liberation from these conditions, i.e., to achieve ultimate union with the divine Ground of all reality, the union of individual *atman* with divine *Brahma*, which is often illustrated as the waters of a river reaching its mouth and dissolving

---

Human Rights: An Interdisciplinary and Interfaith Study, edited by Alan Falconer (Dublin: Irish School of Ecumenics, 1980), 34ff.

[99]   Cf. Abdullah Ahmed An-Naim, "Quran, Sharia and Human Rights: Foundations, Deficiencies and Prospects," in *The Ethics of World Religions and Human Rights*, 61ff. For a recent analysis of this problem, see Christine Schirrmacher, "Islamic Human Rights Declarations and Their Critics," in *International Journal for Religious Freedom*, 4/2011, 37ff.

[100] Cf. Nikki Keddie, "The Rights of Women in Contemporary Islam," in *Human Rights and the World's Religions*, edited by Leroy Rouner (Notre Dame: University of Notre Dame Press, 1988), 76ff. See also Miriam Cooke and Bruce Lawrence, "Muslim Women between Human Rights and Islamic Norms," in *Religious Diversity and Human Rights*, edited by Irene Bloom, J. Paul Martin, and Wayne Proudfoot (New York: Columbia University Press, 1996), 313ff.

[101] Cf. especially *The Universal Islamic Declaration of Human Rights* (1981 Paris) and *The Declaration on Human Rights in Islam* (1990 Cairo).

[102] For a general summary of the issues see Muddathir Abd Al-Rahim, *Human Rights and the World's Major Religions: The Islamic Tradition* (London: Praeger Perspectives, 2005).

themselves in the waters of the ocean. The human individual, i.e., the "subject" of human rights, is viewed as a temporary entity determined by the current state of his or her *karma* and is understood as an intermediate stage in spiritual development, a stage to be overcome and left behind. The divine ground of human beingness can be viewed as a foundation of a specifically Hindu understanding of human dignity, sanctity of human life, and value of each individual.[103] The Hindu tradition therefore contains elements supporting what in the West is called human rights.[104] On the other hand, the sacred texts of Hinduism contain views that are in obvious tension with human rights as they are generally understood (for example, the caste system, the social status of women, the status of untouchables).[105] This is naturally caused by the fact that the Hindu tradition has a very specific understanding of humanity (of what it means to be human), only partially compatible with the anthropology of the 1948 UN declaration.[106]

The same is true about Buddhism. Its basic teaching about the human condition, its main problem and the proposed solution for this problem, has very practical consequences. The individual self – as the "subject" of human rights – actually "does not exist." The empirical self is an illusion; it is a self-deception. And this self-deception, moreover, is one of the major obstacles and barriers on the way to spiritual liberation (reaching Nirvana). At the same time, all human beings (actually all sentient creatures) are, according to Buddhist ontology, mutually dependent and interconnected, and all of them are on their way to ultimate liberation from omnipresent suffering. The most important Buddhist virtue is compassion (*karuna*) – compassion with all sentient and, therefore, suffering beings. This compassion is a powerful motivation for sacrificial care for others. Moreover, Buddha rejected the unjust Hindu stratification of society (caste system). It should not be surprising, therefore, that in Buddhist history we find many admirable examples of defending what we call today human

---

[103] Cf. Kana Mitra, "Human Rights in Hinduism," in *Human Rights in Religious Traditions,* edited by A. Swidler, 77ff. See also Carrie Gustafson, "Gandhi's Philosophy of *Satyagraha*: Cautionary Notes for the International Penal Lobby," in *Religion and Human Rights: Competing Claims?* 88ff.

[104] Cf. John Carman, "Duties and Rights in Hindu Society," in *Human Rights and the World's Religions,* 113 ff; see also Joseph Elder, "Hindu Perspectives on the Individual and the Collectivity," in *Religious Diversity and Human Rights,* 54ff.

[105] See especially the monograph by Arvind Sharma, *Hinduism and Human Rights* (Oxford: Oxford University Press, 2003).

[106] For a general summary of issues involved, see Harold Coward, *Human Rights and the World's Major Religions: The Hindu Tradition* (London: Praeger Perspectives, 2005).

rights: e.g., emancipation of women, care for the poor and for ill people.[107] On the other hand, Buddhist teaching has sometimes been interpreted to imply that outward conditions of human life actually do not matter. It is therefore not necessary to reform unjust social structures and fight against abuses of power and human rights violations, because what is really important (the spiritual liberation of human beings) is actually independent of the outward circumstances of human existence.[108] In Buddhist history, this indifference toward social conditions has led to much passivity and to a lack of engagement in facing the structural evils in society.

Again, as was the case with Islam and Hinduism, we see in Buddhism a very specific anthropology, which has a very significant, yet not quite complete, overlap with the implicit understanding of humanity to be found in the 1948 UN Declaration and subsequent documents.[109] As we have seen, religious and cultural plurality is a serious challenge for the universal validity and applicability of human rights, especially if these rights are presented as anchored in a specifically Judeo-Christian understanding of humanity. Many critics coming from non-European cultural and religious backgrounds naturally see human rights as formulated in the UN documents as culturally particular (Western, Euro-American, and Judeo-Christian), and they often criticize their implicit "Western individualism" as a cultural value that cannot be translated and applied in non-European contexts shaped by different religious and cultural values.[110]

It seems obvious that if we as Christians want to make an effective public case for universal human rights and if we want to join forces with all people of good will, be they Hindu, Buddhist, Muslim, or secular, we have to look for a common language with those who do not share our Christian presuppositions. We have to search for a generally acceptable normative view of humanity as a shared platform for communication and

---

107 Robert Thurman, "Human Rights and Human Responsibilities: Buddhist Views on Individualism and Altruism," in *Religious Diversity and Human Rights*, 87ff. See also Taitetsu Unno, "Personal Rights and Contemporary Buddhism," in *Human Rights and the World's Religions*, 129ff.
108 See K. Inada, "The Buddhist Perspective on Human Rights," in *Human Rights in Religious Traditions*, 66ff., and Sulak Sivaraksa, "Human Rights in the Context of Global Problem-Solving: A Buddhist Perspective," in *The Ethics of World Religions and Human Rights*, 79ff.
109 For a general summary of issues involved, see Robert E. Florida, *Human Rights and the World's Major Religions: The Buddhist Tradition* (London: Praeger Perspectives, 2005).
110 Cf. Stackhouse, "Sources and Prospects for Human Rights Ideas: A Christian Perspective," 183ff.

cooperation with people of other faiths or of no faith. And here I see a major problem in Komárková's proposal.

The key question in relation to Komárková's approach to human rights and their universal validity is the following: Should we as Christians, as we try to make a public claim for human rights and religious freedom, just witness, proclaim, and "preach" our understanding of humanity, based on biblical texts, without any attempt to make it intelligible and plausible for those who do not share our faith? Or should we, in light of cultural and religious pluralism, try to identify and formulate trans-cultural, trans-contextual, universally acceptable norms of human behavior and criteria of humanity?

There is a danger, I think, that if we just insist on the essential tie between Christianity and human rights (which I think we should), without ever trying to show that they make good sense even without explicit reference to the Bible, the claim for their universal validity will be seriously weakened, and we may actually end up leaving the victims of human rights violations in non-Christian societies in the hands of their oppressors. These oppressors will naturally insist that if human rights and the corresponding notion of religious freedom are Christian, they only apply to Christians. Those who are in positions of power can always refer to all sorts of cultural and religious particularities of their society and thereby avoid any accountability for their exercise of injustice or for denying the religious freedom of their subjects. It seems obvious that the contemporary world needs trans-cultural, publicly debatable, universally binding, normative principles of human behavior and criteria of humanity, which would make sense for Hindus, Buddhists, Christians, and even Atheists – in order to protect potential victims of injustice.[111] And in this particular respect, Komárková's view of human rights and their universal validity is deficient, I think, especially in comparison with an alternative view of a Christian approach to human rights as proposed by Thomas K. Johnson, to whose analysis I now turn.

Thomas K. Johnson: the relation between human rights and the natural moral law

Thomas K. Johnson is an Anglo-Saxon Calvinist Protestant theologian, i.e., he belongs exactly to the tradition to which Komárková refers in her analysis of the origin and essence of human rights. Yet his perspective is

---

[111] Cf. Stackhouse, "Sources and Prospects for Human Rights Ideas: A Christian Perspective," 192ff.

different. He agrees with Komárková in emphasizing the Christian origin of universal human rights discourse and a decisive influence of Christianity in its development. He also agrees with her that for Christians, human rights need to be anchored theologically, i.e., with reference to God as their transcendent guarantee.[112] Yet Johnson disagrees with Komárková on one very important point, related to the basis on which we (as Christians) make public claim for the universal validity and applicability of human rights. For Johnson, it is very important for Christians to make an understandable public case for human rights without only referring to the Bible to substantiate their argument.[113] He is convinced that Christians have to formulate their view of human rights in a way that makes sense for believers of other faiths as well as for nonbelievers. There is one tradition of Christian ethical discourse, as Johnson points out, which offers suitable conceptual tools for demonstrating universal relevance and applicability of Christian moral values outside of the Christian church, namely, natural law ethics.[114]

There has been much debate and misunderstanding concerning the question whether and in what sense Christian ethics should use the notion of universal God-given natural moral law.[115] Whereas Roman Catholic theologians seem, by and large, quite comfortable with the notion of a God-given natural moral law, based on the doctrine of creation, many Protestant thinkers, including Božena Komárková, have argued strongly against basing Christian ethical claims on natural law, a concept they view as theologically questionable and actually alien to a "biblical way of thinking."[116] Komárková also claims that natural law is an "illusion," because

---

[112]   Johnson, "Human Rights and Christian Ethics," 326.

[113]   Johnson, *Natural Law Ethics*, chapters 1 and 5; see also "Human Rights and Christian Ethics," 334, and "Biblical Principles in the Public Square," MBS Text 108 (2008), 4, 17ff, available here: https://www.bucer.de/ressource/details/mbs-texte-108-2008-biblical-principles-in-the-public-square.html.

[114]   See Johnson's monograph *Natural Law Ethics: An Evangelical Proposal* (Bonn: VKW, 2005); see also his "The Twofold Work of God," 4.

[115]   Cf. the following recent literature on theological legitimacy of the concept of natural moral law: Stephen J. Grabill, *Rediscovering the Natural Law in Reformed Theological Ethics* (Grand Rapids: Eerdmans, 2006); J. Daryl Charles, *Retrieving the Natural Law: A Return to Moral First Things* (Grand Rapids: Eerdmans, 2008); David VanDrunen, *Natural Law and the Two Kingdoms: A Study in the Development of Reformed Social Thought* (Grand Rapids: Eerdmans, 2010); Robert C. Baker and Roland Cap Ehlke (eds), *Natural Law: A Lutheran Reappraisal*, (Saint Louis: Concordia, 2011); and Jesse Covington, Bryan McGraw, and Micah Watson (eds), *Natural Law and Evangelical Political Theory*, (Lanham, MD: Lexington, 2012.)

[116]   Komárková, "Natural Law and Christianity," in HRRSA, p. 48.

each society has defined what is "natural" very differently.[117] Moreover, Komárková views the notion of natural law as typical of "Roman Catholic scholasticism,"[118] as anchored in a questionable static metaphysical and cosmological framework[119] and as basically incompatible with a biblical worldview and Protestant Christianity.[120]

For these theological reasons, Komárková is convinced that it is a serious mistake for Christians to try to base their claim for universal human rights on natural law.[121] I think it can be demonstrated that Komárková's judgments concerning natural law are not quite justified, or in other words, that these judgments are only justified in relation to certain types of natural law reasoning, which is exactly what Johnson is demonstrating in his analysis of the relation of natural law and Christian ethics. He shows quite convincingly that the sort of arguments Komárková and some other Protestant thinkers present against natural law only apply to a particular kind of natural law concept.[122] If natural law is not viewed as an abstract principle unrelated to God's activity or as an immanent law independent of God, but if it is instead anchored theologically in the framework of the dynamic relation between God and humanity, in the doctrine of creation and the unity of humankind under God's sovereign rule, and especially in relation to the classical theological notion of general revelation, there seems to be no reason to reject this concept and thereby to weaken the public claim of universal applicability and validity of Christian moral values, especially those that underlie universal human rights and the corresponding notion of religious freedom.[123]

Someone might object that this theological understanding of natural moral law anchored in the Christian doctrine of creation and general revelation is open to the same sort of criticism as is Komárková's position, namely, that it is offering a particularist (i.e., biblical) foundation for a universalist claim, unintelligible for those outside the community of Christian faith. But we have to distinguish two different discourses with two different

[117] Komárková, "Natural Law and Christianity," 43, 45.
[118] Komárková, "Natural Law and Christianity," 41; see also her "Human Rights and Christianity," HRRSA, 70.
[119] Komárková, "Natural Law and Christianity," 44.
[120] Komárková, "Natural Law and Christianity," 46.
[121] Komárková, "Natural Law and Christianity," 50.
[122] See Johnson, *Natural Law Ethics*, chapters 1 and 2.
[123] See Johnson, *Natural Law Ethics*, chapter 5; also "Human Rights and Christian Ethics," 334; and his "Christ and Culture," *Evangelical Review of Theology* 35/1, 2011, 14f, available here: https://www.academia.edu/40734562/Christ_and_Culture_2011_edition_for_the_World_Evangelical_Alliance.

audiences (and two different sets of criteria): one is the internal debate among Christian theologians about legitimate biblical and theological foundations of a particular notion (natural moral law in this case); the other is the public debate about human rights and religious freedom in which Christians participate together with people of other faiths and of no faith. In the first debate, reference to creation and general revelation makes sense and is, in fact, necessary. In the second debate, criteria of intelligibility and validity are different. Instead of referring to the particular doctrines of Christian revelation, reference to empirical evidence, to common sense, to generally accessible knowledge, and to universally accepted values such as human dignity are to be used to support one's arguments.

In other words, if Christians want to make a convincing public claim for universal human rights and for the corresponding notion of religious freedom, it does not seem to be enough to just refer to the Bible, especially if we want to invite all people of good will (Hindus, Buddhists, Jews, Muslims, Atheists), not just fellow Christians, to join hands in fighting against human rights violations and in supporting religious freedom in the contemporary world. I am convinced that the notion of natural law provides a meaningful conceptual framework for making an effective, understandable, and plausible public claim for universal human rights, a claim that, unlike some other Christian public claims in this area, cannot be dismissed by pointing to the fact that historically, it is derived from one particular sacred text of one particular faith and therefore does not seem to apply to people who base their lives on different sacred texts or on no sacred text at all.[124] This claim is not weakened by the fact that in the internal Christian debate, Christian theologians have to base the notion of natural moral law on biblical doctrines of creation and general revelation. Why? Because the notion of natural moral law can be easily adapted by people of different cultural and religious backgrounds and can serve as a shared platform for communication, peaceful coexistence, and cooperation. And we need such a platform. And the fact that each religious and cultural tradition will have a different and tradition-specific substantiation of that platform does not make its functioning impossible.

Natural moral law and Christian public defense of human rights

The strength of natural law ethics is its reference to common sense, to generally accessible knowledge, to trans-cultural criteria of value and meaning, to observable general principles, as these can be supported by

---

[124] See Johnson, *Natural Law Ethics*, 88ff.

empirical research[125] and can also be found in all cultural and religious traditions,[126] in other words, its reference to what Christian theology calls
general revelation. There are certain kinds of behavior that are obviously
incompatible with humanity. Always and everywhere. And this fact should
not be dismissed by referring to cultural differences. Christian natural law
ethics has the immense advantage that it can be argued for publicly, it can
be supported by research and empirical evidence and defended in the public square, it can be formulated in universally understandable language,
and therefore it cannot be silenced by referring to its Christian origin or
bias.[127]

This is the reason why I find Božena Komarková's appeal to universal
human rights vulnerable and Thomas Johnson's argumentation more convincing. As Johnson points out, the Bible and the Reformers do, in fact,
teach the doctrine of general revelation, i.e., an awareness of God and his
will and his moral law, available at least to some degree to all people and
at all times and places.[128] As Johnson reminds his readers to make this point
clear, the prophets in ancient Israel do not teach the non-Israelite nations
what is right and what is wrong (as if these nations did not know); they, in
fact, presuppose that these nations know the difference but do not act accordingly.[129] Moreover, drawing on Max Weber's sociological and cultural
analyses, Johnson points out that religion can, in fact, provide or inspire
values that gain general acceptance and have far-reaching influence outside the religious community, and biblical religion can provide such influential values to public cultures *precisely when the biblical values correspond
closely with God's general revelation of the moral law.* Christians should consciously use this sociological/theological observation in their active in-
volvement in public debates on human rights and religious freedom.[130]

---

[125] Cf. Johnson, *Natural Law Ethics*, 75ff.
[126] Cf. Johnson, *Natural Law Ethics*, 85ff.
[127] Johnson, "Human Rights and Christian Ethics," 334.
[128] Cf. Johnson, *Natural Law Ethics*, 131ff; *Human Rights: A Christian Primer*, 47ff; "The
Spirit of the Protestant Work Ethic and the World Economic Crisis," MBS Text 137
(2009), 8f; "The Twofold Work of God in the World," 3ff, and "The Protester, the
Dissident, and the Christian," MBS Text 168 (2012), 3f. Cf. also his "Law and Gospel:
The Hermeneutical/Homiletical Key to Reformation Theology and Ethics," *Evangelical Review of Theology,* 36/2, 2012, 153f.
[129] Johnson, *Natural Law Ethics,* p. 141ff; see also his "The Protester, the Dissident, and
the Christian," p. 5, and "Biblical Principles in the Public Square," p. 5ff. See also
his "Christ and Culture," p. 14ff, and "Law and Gospel: The Hermeneutical/Homi-
letical Key to Reformation Theology and Ethics," p. 159.
[130] In a book published after this article was written, Johnson has argued that people
have an awareness of human dignity as a result of God's general revelation and

I think it is obvious that in the context of contemporary cultural and religious pluralism, Johnson's proposal to base the Christian public claim for biblical moral values and for universal validity of human rights on the God-given natural moral law (anchored – for Christians – in the doctrine of creation and general revelation) offers a more promising platform for public debate and intercultural dialogue and cooperation than does Komárková's appeal to the Christian roots of human rights accompanied with a strict rejection of the notion of natural law. I think it is vitally important for contemporary Christians to be able to present their ethical convictions in ways that are intelligible and hopefully acceptable for non-Christians, in other words, in ways that make it clear that their plausibility does not stand and fall with accepting the Christian faith and its sacred book. I think it is necessary for contemporary Christians, as they strive to fight for human rights and religious freedom, to join hands with all people of good will, not just with fellow Christians. And I think that the sort of ethical theory proposed by Johnson can serve as a suitable and theologically sound platform for such an alliance, based on shared values and concerns. I don't think Komárková's view of human rights and natural law offers such a platform.

Moreover, if we look carefully into the sacred books and traditions of non-Christian religions, we find much evidence supporting Johnson's perspective. In spite of many above-mentioned differences in the areas of metaphysics and religiously defined anthropology, ethical guidelines and moral values tend to be quite similar across all religious traditions.[131] There is actually much more commonality among world religions in the area of ethical values and ideals than in the area of the theological doctrines and metaphysical concepts which substantiate those ideals and values.

In all existing world religions we find some version of the so-called Golden Rule. Moreover, the rules of interpersonal relationships as they are defined in all existing world religions agree generally with the principles

---

that even if suppressed from consciousness, this awareness continues to impinge upon human consciousness and culture. See Johnson, *The First Step in Mission Training: How Our Neighbors Are Wrestling with God's General Revelation* (Bonn: VKW, 2014), p. 21. This provides the condition necessary for a regard for human rights to gain influence within cultures that are not yet shaped by the Judeo-Christian tradition.

[131]   See on this point a classical presentation of those similarities in C. S. Lewis, *The Abolition of Man* (Glasgow: Collins, 1978), and also the very influential statement of the same claim in Hans Küng, *Global Responsibility* (New York: Crossroad Pub., 1991). Komárková tends to neglect or underestimate this trans-cultural consensus in the area of moral values by claiming, as she does, that each society defines what is morally "natural" very differently. It is not quite true, I think.

of the second half of the biblical Decalogue. This relatively far-reaching consensus among world religions in the area of ethical values and ideals has been acknowledged and officially confirmed in documents such as the Declaration Toward a Global Ethic approved by the Parliament of World Religions in Chicago in 1993.[132] I think that the most plausible explanation for this universal consensus from a Christian perspective is the theological understanding of God-given natural moral law, anchored in the doctrine of creation and general revelation.

To summarize, in the global situation of cultural and religious pluralism, I find Johnson's proposal to develop a publicly understandable Christian natural law ethics based on the doctrine of creation and general revelation, which can be supported by empirical evidence, generally accessible knowledge, and appeal to common sense, to provide a suitable platform for cooperation with all people of good will. Johnson's theological/philosophical framework can be viewed as theologically sound within the Christian community and, at the same time, publicly intelligible for claiming the universal validity of human rights globally. This includes the right for religious freedom. Johnson's proposal is more convincing than is the alternative proposal of Božena Komárková, precisely because she refuses to relate her Christian claim for human rights to a universally human normative basis of morality such as the natural moral law. This leaves her with no basis which could serve as a plausible and acceptable platform of dialogue and cooperation, not just for Christians but also for people who do not share the Christian faith.

---

[132] *Declaration Toward a Global Ethic, Parliament of the World's Religions.* Chicago, 1993; https://parliamentofreligions.org/.

Postscript by Thomas K. Johnson:

Human Rights, Control Beliefs, and Spiritual Warfare

Unlike animals, humans defend their violence with words. Even though human dignity is a primordial reality known to all, the twentieth century provided a constant stream of philosophical theories and political ideologies that justified terrible abuses of human beings: fascism, national socialism, Soviet communism, Maoism, functionalism, extreme moral relativism. Some religions were tragically involved in this mix, even proclaiming inhuman ideologies, somewhat rarely sounding a warning trumpet when a truly spiritual response was urgent.[133] There may be a change in our still young and very religious twenty-first century: we see a constant stream of religious extremisms around the globe, sometimes mixing with nationalist extremisms, wreaking havoc on the human race.[134] The threat to humanity from dysfunctional and dangerous religions is making the theological ethics taught in religious communities more important than ever.[135]

We must talk about a battle, a constant spiritual battle, between attacks on human rights and defenses of human rights. To be more pointed, this is a constant war for and against ordinary people and their futures, not just about abstract rights. The physical battle may be in the streets, prisons, refugee camps, courts, or slavery brothels; behind the visible battle there is war in the highest places, in "the heavens."

Jews, Christians, and Muslims are familiar with a war between Satan's followers and the angels who are loyal to God. The story is told to enlist humans to join the war on the side of the angels. When the apostle Paul took up this theme, he mentioned several categories of enemies. "Our struggle is not against flesh and blood, but against the rulers, against the authorities, against the powers of this dark world and against the spiritual

---

[133] As one example, the so-called "German Christian movement" of the 1930s used Christian terminology and institutions to promote the political agenda of Adolf Hitler.

[134] One could mention ISIS and Hindu nationalism as examples.

[135] Within Christianity there were texts on theological ethics that supported Hitler, as well as theological texts that exposed the evil of National Socialism and its ideology. Within Islam there are texts on theological ethics that support terrorism and religious texts that expose the evil of terrorism.

forces of evil in the heavenly realms" (Ephesians 6:12). When we read of the conflict-filled life of Paul, we see him not only wrestling with devils and archdemons; we also see him fighting against ideas and beliefs that control and destroy people. "See to it that no one takes you captive through hollow and deceptive philosophy, which depends on human tradition and the elemental spiritual forces of this world," he wrote (Colossians 2:8). Overcoming captivity to "deceptive philosophy" is part of spiritual warfare.

When psychologists discuss control beliefs, they are generally considering the extent to which people believe they can control their own lives and their futures. However, some philosophers use the term *control beliefs* in a way that is almost the opposite, to describe beliefs that control people. Beliefs of this rank, perhaps held unconsciously, control not only what people do but also everything else people allow themselves to believe. Nicholas Wolterstorff argued, "Everyone who weighs a theory has certain beliefs as to what constitutes an acceptable *sort* of theory on the matter under consideration. We can call these *control* beliefs . . . Control beliefs function in two ways. Because we hold them we are led to *reject* certain sorts of theories . . . On the other hand control beliefs also lead us to *devise* theories."[136] As Wolterstorff and similar thinkers have argued, the historical religions frequently function as control beliefs, though many cosmological, historical, ideological, or scientific convictions also can function as control beliefs, even if people do not always recognize which beliefs are controlling them.[137]

---

[136]   Nicholas Wolterstorff, *Reason within the Bounds of Religion* (Grand Rapids: Eerdmans, 1976), 63-64. The title of this book makes clear the author's intent to reverse the understanding of the Enlightenment claim regarding the proper relation between faith and reason summarized in Immanuel Kant's *Religion within the Limits of Reason Alone*, published in German in 1793 (German title: *Die Religion innerhalb der Grenzen der bloßen Vernunft*). While the technical details of Kant's theory of knowledge were only understood by philosophers, his broader contribution to Western culture reflected that of the Enlightenment more broadly, that all religious claims should be evaluated by reason. Wolterstorff is one of the twentieth-century thinkers who argues that this Enlightenment claim ignores important facts about human beings, one of which is that what people regard as reason, rationality, or science is always controlled by other influences and beliefs, including religious beliefs.

[137]   Charles Taylor uses the term "epistemological story" in a way that approximates what Wolterstorff means with the term "control belief." Taylor writes, "Once the epistemological story is properly in place . . . it becomes part of the unquestioned background, something whose shape is not perceived, but which conditions,

A serious look at human rights reveals a hurricane of confusion; activists and writers are controlled by all sorts of belief, unbelief, and misbelief. Such beliefs are spiritual forces, sometimes evil spiritual forces, functioning as controlling authorities in institutions, movements, and documents. Following the apostle Paul, we have to say our struggle is not against flesh and blood; it is a spiritual battle for human rights, sometimes against the beliefs controlling the discussion and application of human rights principles.

One of the crucial steps needed to repower the human rights movement is for people of authentic faith to engage in spiritual warfare on behalf of human rights. This will require prayer but also discernment of ideas and values. We need to reduce the power of the ideas that hinder the protection of defenseless people and increase the power of the ideas that protect the image of divine dignity in the other.

Links to related materials for further study:

Thomas K. Johnson, *Human Rights: A Christian Primer,* 2nd ed., The WEA Global Issues Series, vol. 1 (Bonn: VKW, 2016), https://www.academia.edu/36884876/Human _Rights_A_Christian_Primer.

Thomas K. Johnson, ed., with Thomas Schirrmacher and Christof Sauer, *Global Declarations on Freedom of Religion or Belief and Human Rights,* The WEA Global Issues Series, vol. 18 (Bonn: VKW, 2017), https://www.academia.edu/36886097/ Global_Declarations_on_Freedom_of_Religion_or_Belief_and_Human_Rights.

Thomas K. Johnson, *Christian Ethics in Secular Cultures,* The WEA Theological Commission World of Theology Series, vol. 2 (Bonn: VKW, 2014), https://www.bucer. org/fileadmin/dateien/Dokumente/Buecher/WoT_2_-_Thomas_K._Johnson_- _Christian_Ethics_in_Secular_Cultures.pdf .

Thomas K. Johnson, *Natural Law Ethics: An Evangelical Proposal* (Bonn: VKW, 2005), https://www.academia.edu/36884239/Natural_Law_Ethics_An_Evangelical_ Proposal

Thomas K. Johnson, "Christ and Culture," *Evangelical Review of Theology* 35:1, 4-16, February 2011, https://www.academia.edu/40734562/Christ_and_Culture_2011 _edition.

Thomas K. Johnson, "Law and Gospel: The Hermeneutical and Homiletical Key to Reformation Theology and Ethics" *Evangelical Review of Theology* 43:1, 53-70, February 2019, https://www.academia.edu/38262994/Law_and_Gospel_Luther_ and_Calvin.

Thomas K. Johnson, "The Rejection of God's Natural Moral Law: Losing the Soul of Western Civilization," *Evangelical Review of Theology* 43:3 243-252, August 2019,

---

largely unnoticed, the way we think, infer, experience, process claims, and arguments." Charles Taylor, *A Secular Age* (Harvard University Press, 2007), 565.

https://www.academia.edu/39590583/The_Rejection_of_Gods_Natural_Moral_
Law_Losing_the_Soul_of_Western_Civilization.

Thomas K. Johnson, "A Case for Ethical Cooperation between Evangelical Christians
and Humanitarian Islam," *Evangelical Review of Theology* 44:3, 204–217, August
2020, https://www.academia.edu/43824423/Humanitarian_Islam_Report_with
_ERT_cover.

Thomas K. Johnson, "Dialogue with Kierkegaard in Protestant Theology: Donald
Bloesch, Francis Schaeffer, and Helmut Thielicke," MBS Text 175 (2013),
https://www.bucer.org/resources/resources/details/mbs-texte-175-2013-dialo
gue-with-kierkegaard-in-protestant-theology-donald-bloesch-francis-scha.html.

Thomas K. Johnson, "The Moral Crisis of the West: Reflections from Helmut Thielicke
and Francis Schaeffer," MBS Text 117 (2009), https://www.academia.edu/
37063806/The_Moral_Crisis_of_the_West_Reflections_from_Helmut_Thielicke
_and_Francis_Schaeffer.

Thomas K. Johnson, "The Twofold Work of God in the World," MBS Text 102 (2008),
https://www.academia.edu/37063867/The_Twofold_Work_of_God_in_the_
World.

Thomas Schirrmacher, *Human Rights: Promise and Reality,* The WEA Global Issues Series,
vol. 15 (Bonn: VKW, 2014); https://iirf.eu/journal-books/global-issues-series/
human-rights-18/.

Thomas Schirrmacher, *Racism,* The WEA Global Issues Series, vol. 8 (Bonn: VKW, 2008),
https://www.iirf.eu/site/assets/files/91879/wea_gis_8_racism_schirrmacher
_01.pdf.

Thomas Schirrmacher, *Human Trafficking: The Return to Slavery,* The WEA Global Issues
Series, Vol. 12 (Bonn: VKW, 2013), https://www.iirf.eu/site/assets/files/
92915/wea_gis_12_-_thomas_schirrmacher_-_human_trafficking.pdf.

Thomas Schirrmacher, *The Persecution of Christians Concerns Us All,* The WEA Global Issues
Series, vol. 5, 3rd edition (Bonn: VKW, 2018), https://www.iirf.eu/site/assets/
files/91406/wea-gis_05_thschirrmacher-persecution_of_christians_3rd_ed.pdf.

Discrimination, Persecution, Martyrdom: Following Christ Together, edited by Huibert van
Beek and Larry Miller, with an introduction by Larry Miller (Bonn: VKW, 2018),
https://globalchristianforum.org/wp-content/uploads/2020/10/Tirana_Repo
rt_DPM_Consultation-1.pdf.

World Evangelical Alliance

World Evangelical Alliance is a global ministry working with local churches around the world to join in common concern to live and proclaim the Good News of Jesus in their communities. WEA is a network of churches in 129 nations that have each formed an evangelical alliance and over 100 international organizations joining together to give a worldwide identity, voice and platform to more than 600 million evangelical Christians. Seeking holiness, justice and renewal at every level of society – individual, family, community and culture, God is glorified and the nations of the earth are forever transformed.

Christians from ten countries met in London in 1846 for the purpose of launching, in their own words, "a new thing in church history, a definite organization for the expression of unity amongst Christian individuals belonging to different churches." This was the beginning of a vision that was fulfilled in 1951 when believers from 21 countries officially formed the World Evangelical Fellowship. Today, 150 years after the London gathering, WEA is a dynamic global structure for unity and action that embraces 600 million evangelicals in 129 countries. It is a unity based on the historic Christian faith expressed in the evangelical tradition. And it looks to the future with vision to accomplish God's purposes in discipling the nations for Jesus Christ.

Commissions:

- Theology
- Missions
- Religious Liberty
- Women's Concerns
- Youth
- Information Technology

Initiatives and Activities

- Ambassador for Human Rights
- Ambassador for Refugees
- Creation Care Task Force
- Global Generosity Network
- International Institute for Religious Freedom
- International Institute for Islamic Studies
- Leadership Institute
- Micah Challenge
- Global Human Trafficking Task Force
- Peace and Reconciliation Initiative
- UN-Team

Church Street Station
P.O. Box 3402
New York, NY 10008-3402
Phone +[1] 212 233 3046
Fax +[1] 646-957-9218
www.worldea.org

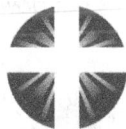

WEA
World Evangelical Alliance

Giving Hands

GIVING HANDS GERMANY (GH) was established in 1995 and is officially recognized as a nonprofit foreign aid organization. It is an international operating charity that – up to now – has been supporting projects in about 40 countries on four continents. In particular we care for orphans and street children. Our major focus is on Africa and Central America. GIVING HANDS always mainly provides assistance for self-help and furthers human rights thinking.

The charity itself is not bound to any church, but on the spot we are co-operating with churches of all denominations. Naturally we also cooperate with other charities as well as governmental organizations to provide assistance as effective as possible under the given circumstances.

The work of GIVING HANDS GERMANY is controlled by a supervisory board. Members of this board are Manfred Feldmann, Colonel V. Doner and Kathleen McCall. Dr. Christine Schirrmacher is registered as legal manager of GIVING HANDS at the local district court. The local office and work of the charity are coordinated by Rev. Horst J. Kreie as executive manager. Dr. theol. Thomas Schirrmacher serves as a special consultant for all projects.

Thanks to our international contacts companies and organizations from many countries time and again provide containers with gifts in kind which we send to the different destinations where these goods help to satisfy elementary needs. This statutory purpose is put into practice by granting nutrition, clothing, education, construction and maintenance of training centers at home and abroad, construction of wells and operation of water treatment systems, guidance for self-help and transportation of goods and gifts to areas and countries where needy people live.

GIVING HANDS has a publishing arm under the leadership of Titus Vogt, that publishes human rights and other books in English, Spanish, Swahili and other languages.

These aims are aspired to the glory of the Lord according to the basic Christian principles put down in the Holy Bible.

Baumschulallee 3a · D-53115 Bonn · Germany
Phone: +49 / 228 / 695531 · Fax +49 / 228 / 695532
www.gebende-haende.de · info@gebende-haende.de

Martin Bucer Seminary

**Faithful to biblical truth
Cooperating with the Evangelical Alliance
Reformed**

Solid training for the Kingdom of God
- Alternative theological education
- Study while serving a church or working another job
- Enables students to remain in their own churches
- Encourages independent thinking
- Learning from the growth of the universal church.

Academic
- For the Bachelor's degree: 180 Bologna-Credits
- For the Master's degree: 120 additional Credits
- Both old and new teaching methods: All day seminars, independent study, term papers, etc.

Our Orientation:
- Complete trust in the reliability of the Bible
- Building on reformation theology
- Based on the confession of the German Evangelical Alliance
- Open for innovations in the Kingdom of God

Our Emphasis:
- The Bible
- Ethics and Basic Theology
- Missions
- The Church

Our Style:
- Innovative
- Relevant to society
- International
- Research oriented
- Interdisciplinary

Structure
- 15 study centers in 7 countries with local partners
- 5 research institutes
- President: Prof. Dr. Thomas Schirrmacher
  Vice President: Prof. Dr. Thomas K. Johnson
- Deans: Thomas Kinker, Th.D.;
  Titus Vogt, lic. theol., Carsten Friedrich, M.Th.

Missions through research
- Institute for Religious Freedom
- Institute for Islamic Studies
- Institute for Life and Family Studies
- Institute for Crisis, Dying, and Grief Counseling
- Institute for Pastoral Care

www.bucer.eu • info@bucer.eu

Berlin I Bielefeld I Bonn I Chemnitz I Hamburg I Munich I Pforzheim

Innsbruck I Istanbul I Izmir I Linz I Prague I São Paulo I Tirana I Zurich